YOUR LIFE IS
DESIGNED
TO WORK

A Psychological and
Spiritual Guide

JANE ILENE COHEN

YOUR LIFE IS DESIGNED TO WORK

A Psychological and Spiritual Guide

Copyright © 2021 by Jane Ilene Cohen

Printed in the United States of America
Conscious Life Press, Encinitas, CA
LifeIsDesignedToWork.com
First Edition

Library of Congress Control Number: 2021915953

ISBN: 978-0-578-96231-3

ACKNOWLEDGMENTS

The NLP (Neuro-Linguistic Programming) basic concept of "limiting decisions," as taught by Dr. Tad James, has been invaluable as a foundation and jumping-off point for developing this thought system. (Although it is not religiously based) this book also uses a modification of the Christian Science synonyms for God as a jumping-off point.

In addition, the NLP perspective that we only experience a model of the world, as opposed to experiencing it directly, also greatly influenced this work, although I took it in a different direction.

The support and input from friends—in particular, Jenny Schipper, Lynn Pollock, and Rebecca Speer—has sustained me in the long process of bringing this book into focus. And, my dear lifelong friend, Judy Rothschild, has been a consistent cheerleader over the years in helping me get this book out.

My very talented editor and writing coach, Jan Allegretti, has been amazing in her ability to help me structure and focus this book so that what it's meant to bring into the world could be heard. My editor, John Cannon, has been wonderful to work with and masterful in his editing, comments, and insights, putting the final polish on my book.

DISCLAIMER

When I refer to "therapy" or "therapy sessions" in this book, I am not referring to traditional therapy, such as practiced by psychotherapists or psychologists. I am referring to NLP TimeLine Counseling sessions, which is what I call the sessions I give.

Time Line Therapy® is an NLP process for therapeutic change created by Dr. Tad James. NLP TimeLine is a process for therapeutic change I developed that integrates my Life Is Designed to Work thought system with the Time Line Therapy® process.

This book is not meant to provide psychological or other individual professional services. If you need personal expert assistance or counseling, you should seek the individual services of a competent professional.

CONTENTS

ACKNOWLEDGMENTS i

DISCLAIMER iii

INTRODUCTION 1

PART ONE: UNDERSTANDING THE PROBLEM 7

CHAPTER ONE: Our Subjective Perception of What Is Real 9

CHAPTER TWO: How Our Perceptions Get Distorted 17

CHAPTER THREE: The Substitute Persona 31

CHAPTER FOUR: What We Choose to Give Our Life Stability .. 43

CHAPTER FIVE: Separation from Our Source 49

CHAPTER SIX: The Alternate Reality We Live In 55

PART TWO: SHIFTING FROM THE SUBSTITUTE TO THE REAL WORLD 75

CHAPTER SEVEN: Defusing Your Emotional Triggers 77

CHAPTER EIGHT: The Real World 97

CHAPTER NINE: Distinguishing between Our Substitute World and the Real World 109

CHAPTER TEN: Life Is for Us 121

CHAPTER ELEVEN: Bringing Yourself into the Present Moment 135

CHAPTER TWELVE: Shifting Your Plumb Line 150

CHAPTER THIRTEEN: Living in the Real World as an Empowered Adult 163

CHAPTER FOURTEEN: Finding Solutions in the Real World .. 175

CHAPTER FIFTEEN: An Overview and Global Perspective 205

PART TWO SUMMARY: Shifting into the Real World 223

GLOSSARY 225

ABOUT THE AUTHOR 231

INTRODUCTION

Realizing life is inherently designed to work took quite a journey.

I was born in July 1945, near the end of an old era. It was just a month before the atomic bombs were released, bringing a cataclysmic end to World War II. Growing up in a Chicago suburb, I couldn't relate to much of mainstream life. Hardly anything made sense to me. It was like making my way through a fog.

In high school, this began to change. It was the early 1960s, and the cultural revolution of the hippies and shifting social standards caught my attention and my imagination. New ways of looking at the world and experiencing life began emerging. I started feeling engaged.

The Importance of Being Here Now

About a decade later, now living in California, I read Richard Alpert's (Ram Dass) book, *Be Here Now*. It had a large impact on me, making clear the importance of coming into the present moment. I spent countless hours trying to be here now. But try as hard as I might, I just couldn't do it.

Then a series of pivotal experiences led to me finally being able to cross that barrier:

The Spiritual Community

In 1971, I joined a small "New Age" spiritual community.

I have always had a strong desire to be a good person, but the spiritual leader judged me (as well as most of the others in the community) as being bad. I bought into the idea that we had to save our souls and, as a result, fully participated in the experiences the spiritual leader set up in the community. It was a confrontational, emotionally painful, stressful, and frightening experience. I stayed there for twenty-two years. (Yes, I really stayed there twenty-two years.)

Often feeling I was failing, I went through many dark nights of the soul, by which I mean times of great emotional despair, not seeing a way forward. During one particularly difficult time, I "made a deal with God": If God got me through what I was going through, I would help other people do the same. Looking back on it, I can see that from that point on, I had more and more of a sense I was meant to be a healer.

I had faced the possibility that I was a bad person and examined it to the bottom. Through that intense, soul-wrenching experience, I eventually realized how mistaken and dysfunctional it is to judge people as good versus bad. I experienced what happens when you ignore your own needs for the "good of the whole." I experienced what happens when you live by sacrifice and by treating others as more worthy than yourself. And I learned what happens when you let others define reality for you. In other words, I learned a lot about what causes life not to work and why.

The situation forced me to come into my own direct experience instead of blindly taking as reality what others said was true. That was the only way I could endure the spiritual community and eventually gain the strength to leave it. I was almost totally not awake when I joined the community and awake to a large degree when I left it. I had begun to be here now.

A Course in Miracles

After leaving the spiritual community, I moved into an apartment and lived by myself for the first time in my life. I was no longer interpreting my experiences from the perspective of mainstream life, having been disconnected from it for twenty-two years. At the same time, having realized how dysfunctional the spiritual community was, I was no longer interpreting my experiences from that perspective either. I was in a sort of limbo state.

That's when I started studying *A Course in Miracles*, which is a very positive spiritual philosophy. I threw myself into an intense study of it, feeling that my life depended on understanding it. Looking back, I realize I was starting to build a positive way of looking at life, around which to interpret my experiences of reality.

NLP and Time Line Therapy® Training

Two years later, I met a woman at a party who was a Neuro-Linguistic Programming (NLP) practitioner. She did Time Line Therapy®, which is an NLP process. What she said about it caught my attention, and I decided to have a session with her.

I was impressed with the Time Line process in the session because it worked directly with how experience is formed. Also, the process felt much more empowering than the traditional therapy I had experienced before. Somehow, I knew this was the direction for my life's work.

Eventually, I found myself on a plane headed to Hawaii to study NLP with Dr. Tad James. Studying NLP with Tad gave me concrete tools that helped me understand how the human psyche works. The most important of these was learning the NLP concept of limiting decisions. I've used this concept as a jumping-off point for much that has unfolded for me as I developed the Life Is Designed to Work thought system.

Taking a Stand on "Life Is Designed to Work"

In 1995, I began my counseling practice.

After studying NLP and *A Course in Miracles*, the most important thing I came away with was the idea that life is designed to work. Even though neither of these disciplines directly says that, it is what stuck with me as their true impact.

When I began working with clients, I held that idea in place. But until I saw the results, I didn't really know it was true. Clients would see me because their lives weren't working in some way. When I facilitated clearing the limiting decisions at the bottom of what wasn't working in their lives (such as I'm not good enough, I'm not valuable, or people can't be trusted), I found that their lives transformed and worked. Their lives shifted, often in ways I couldn't have predicted. Conflicts would resolve, their finances would turn around, or they would stop finding themselves in dysfunctional relationships.

I'm describing this because it shows where the real problem is. Most of us experience many of the problems in our lives as being caused by outside factors we can't control (such as the economy, our landlord, or the nature of men or women).

4

But the results of releasing limiting decisions made it clear to me that our problems are rarely about anything outside ourselves. Instead, it is our own limiting decisions that distort our experience of reality. (I explain in depth what limiting decisions are in Chapter Two.)

When I took a stand on the principle that life is designed to work, it felt as though I walked through a portal in which a new way of perceiving reality became available to me. I started tapping into a body of knowledge I hadn't previously been aware of. It was beyond what I had learned from NLP, as well as all my previous studies and life experiences.

I've been tapping into and have been inspired by that body of knowledge since 1995. That knowledge is the Life Is Designed to Work thought system I am teaching in this book and is central to all the work I do.

This thought system holds in place a particular perspective on how life works. It structures and focuses the knowledge and experiences I bring to this book from nearly thirty years of working with clients in counseling sessions, workshops, and transformational groups.

In this book, I draw on these years of direct experience with how the human psyche, emotions, spirit, and evolutionary process work. This book is also based on my present-moment, day-to-day observations in the world as I live my own life. A lot of my understanding that life is designed to work is based on my ability to come into present-moment experience (which I finally became able to do) and shed light on what we are all aware of but haven't understood.

This book shows you how to find a way forward regardless of your life's circumstances. It gives you a way to understand your experiences so you can more effectively move toward a life that increasingly works.

PART ONE

UNDERSTANDING
THE PROBLEM

CHAPTER ONE

Our Subjective Perception of What Is Real

Imagine yourself moving through your day.

Your life may be going well, or it may not be. Maybe it's somewhere in between.

Perhaps you mostly feel happy. Your relationships and your work (or means of support) are going well. You usually feel connected with yourself and in tune with your life. And, like most of us, there are also times when your life isn't going as well. Maybe you sometimes get upset by certain people or circumstances and lose that sense of well-being.

Or perhaps your life isn't going well in general. Maybe you feel stressed about your job and your finances. Or maybe you have (or someone close to you has) major health challenges. Or maybe you keep getting into relationships that don't work. Or maybe you feel upset by what's happening in the larger world around you.

More and more, our world seems out of control in ways that used to only touch us indirectly. Now the effects are becoming increasingly more personal to us. Climate change has gone from an abstract idea you hear about in the news to heat waves and wild weather patterns you are actually living through. Terrorism has gone from something that only affects faraway countries to something much closer to home.

As this book is being written, we are in the midst of the COVID-19 pandemic. Its effects have upended our lives and threatened our well-being and survival on a personal and global level.

Regardless of the times, when life experiences are difficult, overwhelming, or feel out of control, you may feel powerless or at a loss. You may experience what happens in life as random or without meaning. Or you may feel that life just plain doesn't work.

And yet, we live with the deep hope and perhaps even conviction that there is meaning in life, and some order can be found. Or at least we want to.

In difficult times, how can we find solid ground to make sense of things in our lives and in the world? How can we experience life as working?

What We Need in Order to Experience Life as Working

Three components are essential:

- <u>Survival</u>: If we're not alive, the rest doesn't matter.

- <u>Well-Being</u>: Well-being is a higher level of survival. Without well-being, we may survive physically but not emotionally, mentally, or spiritually. To have well-being, we must not just survive. We must thrive.

- **Stability**: Having stability means we have a steady source to orient ourselves around. It keeps us in balance regardless of what might come our way. When we have a stable source for our survival and well-being, we experience life as working.

Your ability to go toward or bring into your life what you need and desire determines whether you survive, have well-being, and have stability. I'm sure you've observed that some of us do well at this, or do well in some areas, while others of us do not.

Maybe you know some people who usually get into good relationships and others who usually find themselves in destructive, unhappy ones. Maybe you know some people who do well financially and others who are always struggling. You probably do well in some areas of your own life and not so well in others.

We spend much of our lives trying to understand how life works so we can have what matters to us: What is the best way to help my child? How can I make ends meet so I can afford what I need? What can I do about my marriage? How do I find friends? What is a dead-end and what is the way forward? What is dangerous and what is safe to go toward? How do I navigate the education system or the government system? It can feel overwhelming.

Do you know people who appear never to be overwhelmed? They have fixed ideas about how the world works, how the people in their lives should behave, how their sister should raise her child, or what the best religion is. For the most part, they don't question or wonder about how life works. They don't question whether their perception of the world around them is true.

Fixed ideas like these can give a person a sense of stability. She (or he) can base decisions on these fixed ideas and orient her life around them. And this may work in her life unless or until some crisis occurs that doesn't fit into her rigid description of what is real. Or this may work until the narrow, limited world she has backed herself into becomes unworkable for her in some way.

Our Subjective Perceptions

Although we may not have such rigid ideas, most of us don't usually question our perception of what is real. That is because our perceptions are the ground we stand on to make sense of our world.

To us, reality is what we see, experience, and feel. We perceive reality as something objective that happens to us. For example: My husband betrayed me when he slept with my best friend, or the pandemic caused my business to fail. To us, this is objective reality.

But when we look more closely at how we define our experience, we can realize we are never experiencing reality directly. We are only experiencing a model of reality. We define reality based on the information our senses pick up and how we interpret that information—not on what is actually there or what is actually happening.

Interpretations are subjective. For example, when your husband slept with your best friend, you probably interpreted his motives for doing it as having a particular meaning to him in relation to you. Depending on how what he did affected you,

you might have thought he wanted to hurt you, he doesn't respect you, he doesn't care about you, or he doesn't desire you. To you, your interpretation is objective reality.

But there are all kinds of things that might be going on in your husband's mind. Perhaps he felt you were no longer interested in him because you no longer seem to want to have sex with him. And he thought having sex with your friend would make you jealous and would make you want him. Or maybe he feels inadequate around you and needed to prove himself. Or he might be in an unconscious state, not aware of why he was doing what he was doing, just acting out of some unconscious pain he was in.

If you approach this situation with your husband from a set, subjective perspective, such as that he is trying to hurt you or is against you in some way, it is unlikely you'll find a positive way through it. This mistaken approach causes life not to work. The conflict and lack of communication between you and your husband will likely get worse, and you'll go in the opposite direction from the love that is really there between you.

Now let's switch to the example where you interpret your business as failing because of the pandemic:

There are many ways to look at this situation. Many businesses haven't failed during the pandemic. It depends on the attitude you bring to the situation. Depending on how resourceful and creative you are, circumstances in the world can be used for or against you.

This situation might have brought to light weak areas in how you have run your business. You could have let this challenging situation motivate you to pay attention to and improve these pivotal areas. Or you might have offered different services that would have been more relevant to your clients in the current circumstances.

Your set interpretation that the pandemic caused your business to fail limits what's possible for you. It could prevent you from learning how to work with economic and social changes in the future.

When you make set interpretations, as in these examples about your husband and your business, and you believe they are objective reality, it closes doors and opportunities for you.

Each of us interprets our experiences moment by moment. We live our lives based on those interpretations. Our interpretations affect the decisions we make and the actions we take. These decisions and actions affect whether our life works or it doesn't.

If you're like most of us, you are unaware that the interpretations you make are not necessarily accurate. You are unaware that these inaccurate interpretations are what have led to many of the difficulties you face in your life.

You are not at fault or to blame for your misinterpretations. The mechanisms that cause misinterpretations are happening on an unconscious level.

Making clear what causes us to misinterpret our experiences and what causes us to live a life that doesn't work well is the focus of the first part of this book.

The second part of the book guides you to an altogether different framework. It guides you to an in-depth understanding and experience of the positive way life actually works. It shows you how to live a life that works. This is supported by exercises to help you transform your experiences in the context of your actual life.

The new framework I'm teaching in this book is called the Life Is Designed to Work thought system.

So now, let's embark on this transformational journey.

CHAPTER TWO

How Our Perceptions Get Distorted

Much of actual reality is beyond what our human senses can detect. In addition, the amount of information we *can* be aware of is massive. This information bombards our senses every moment in every situation or experience. It would be impossible to take it all in. By necessity, we filter out most of it.

What information you filter in and how you interpret it is subjective and happens on an unconscious level. In a split second, your unconscious mind decides what is relevant to you, allows it in, and makes an interpretation of what it means. These filtered-in pieces of information are what define your model of reality.

Actual Reality Does Exist

Regardless of what you filter in or out, and regardless of your subjective interpretations, actual reality does exist. Your ability to perceive what is real greatly impacts your ability (or lack of ability) to survive, have stability, and well-being.

Without enough awareness of what is real, you can't accurately distinguish between what is safe and what is dangerous; you can't find real love, as opposed to obsession or manipulation; and you can't figure out the way forward versus what is a dead-end. Without enough awareness of what is real, you have no true basis for anything you decide to do in life.

How aware you are of what is real depends on the particular information you filter in or block out and how accurately you interpret the information you filter in.

Limiting Decisions

"Limiting decisions" have a lot to do with what information you filter in or out and how you interpret it. They are decisions made in childhood, such as I am bad, I am not valuable, I am a failure, or people can't be trusted, and are made on an unconscious level. They are always some form of deciding that life doesn't work and usually that there is something inherently wrong with you. They are called limiting because they end up narrowing the options you have in life.

Limiting decisions are never true. They are mistaken interpretations of your experience and distort your perception of what is real. They are the root of whatever isn't working well in your life, such as relationship problems, financial troubles, low self-esteem, depression, or anxiety.

Limiting decisions are usually formed before the age of six or seven and sometimes in adolescence. They get formed when something traumatic or overwhelming happens in your life. Because of the limited amount of development and the lack of experience you had at that young age, you can't make conscious sense of what happened. Your perception of reality is shattered. You enter a state of chaos and confusion—a state

18

of shock. Your conscious mind stops functioning, and your unconscious mind takes over. (By "unconscious mind," I mean the aspect of the mind that isn't in our conscious control and doesn't have conscious awareness.) This creates a state of trance.

In this hypnotic state, you dissociate yourself from this experience you are unable to make sense of. You replace it with a limiting decision that redefines the meaning of that experience for you. It is a simplified interpretation based on your limited experience and understanding of life.

Because you are dissociated from the traumatic experience, the people and circumstances in that experience become symbols to you rather than who or what they actually are. These symbols are in the form of generalized categories, such as the man who has the power, a stranger, or the woman you are dependent on. As a result, limiting decisions are made in relation to general categories rather than about a specific person or circumstance.

Let's say that in reaction to something your mother did, you make a limiting decision that she can't be trusted. Your mother represents to you the woman you are dependent on. So, instead of deciding that your mother can't be trusted in this moment, you decide any woman you're dependent on can't be trusted. Examples of other women who fit into that category might be your teacher or your sister. It could even be someone you're only dependent on for a moment or in a particular situation, such as a clerk in a store.

When you make a limiting decision about yourself, you are also dissociated from yourself. Your limiting decision becomes generalized into the nature of who you are rather than about a specific behavior that occurred at a specific moment. For example, rather than deciding "I did a stupid thing," you decide "I am a stupid person." It's a sweeping generalization about the nature of who you are.

Here's an example of how a limiting decision is formed:

Mary grew up in an authoritarian household in which her father was clearly in charge. Everything had to be done his way. Mary's mother rarely contradicted him. When she did, she was careful to couch it in self-deprecating words.

Although Mary had little contact with her father, who wasn't much interested in children, she learned the rules he set up and followed them.

One day, when Mary was five years old, she found a hurt little bird and brought it home to take care of it. Her father saw the bird and yelled, "How dare you bring that disgusting thing into my house!" He demanded that Mary get rid of it immediately.

Mary was afraid the bird wouldn't live if she left it outside, so she sneaked it into her room when her father wasn't looking. Later that day, Mary's father went to her room to tell her to do something. He found Mary there with her bird. His face turned red, and his eyes had a scary look Mary hadn't seen before. He pulled Mary out of her room by her hair and yelled, "You ungrateful, horrible girl! I told you to get rid of that filthy bird! How dare you disobey me!" And he pulled off his belt and whipped her with it.

Mary's head was spinning. She couldn't consciously grasp what had happened. The violence of his actions knocked the wind out of her. She was in a state of terror, confusion, and shock. Her sense of reality was deeply shaken and destabilized. She no longer had the sense that she knew what was real.

When Mary went into a state of shock, her unconscious mind took over, and she made limiting decisions based on her limited experience and understanding of life.

Since her father's violence was in reaction to what she did, and he called her "horrible girl," Mary decided she must be bad. She also decided that men she's dependent on (as represented by her father) are dangerous to her. Making those decisions gave Mary a way to explain to herself why her father reacted the way he did.

Like all of us, when we made our limiting decisions, Mary didn't have the perspective to realize she lacked experience and development. She thought her interpretation of this event was reality.

How Limiting Decisions Distort Your Experience of What Is Real

When you experience a traumatic event, it is by definition frightening. But the most frightening aspect of the experience is that it destabilizes your sense of what is real. This leaves you disoriented and makes it difficult for you to function.

Making a limiting decision enables you to regain your sense of a stable reality because it gives you the sense that you know what just happened and why.

However, since limiting decisions are never true, you will likely encounter life circumstances that challenge the truth of your limiting decisions, jeopardizing this stability. To maintain stability, your unconscious mind functions like a background computer program, just looking for excuses to prove the limiting decision is true.

It filters in information that would prove your limiting decision is true and filters out anything that might disprove it. This process also affects the kinds of people and situations you attract to yourself or are attracted to, depending on whether they confirm your limiting decision. In addition, this affects how you interpret experiences that occur in your life.

You have now created a distorted model of reality that has become your objective reality. This distorted model alters your perception of what is real on a fundamental level. It becomes the foundation of the stability of your daily experience (in the areas of your life affected by your limiting decisions). It is now the reality you are standing on from which you make sense of your world.

Even if you have conscious awareness that there is something wrong with how you view reality, this distorted model still unconsciously structures your experience. In our example with Mary, when she gets older, she is aware she has a problem with the kind of men she chooses to get into a relationship with and tries to choose differently. Despite that, she ends up with men who sooner or later become abusive.

This is because Mary now believes all men she could potentially depend on (such as in an intimate relationship) are dangerous. For that reason, she no longer thinks she has a real choice about men. As a result, when she gets older, she only recognizes men with a similar abusive pattern as being potential intimate relationships. From within this limited range, she tries to make the best choice she can.

Mary unconsciously sets up her world to reinforce this perception of reality by becoming friends with women who have had similar experiences with men. They gossip about how men can't be trusted, and they commiserate about the most recent wrong they have endured—reinforcing this perspective of men in each other.

Although that original situation with her father is no longer happening, Mary has continued to recreate it, on an unconscious level, from that original moment on.

When we were children, each of us made limiting decisions in reaction to traumatic or overwhelming events. Each time we made one, we believed reality was imposing itself on us. The truth is *we* were projecting our limited experience onto *reality*. Each time we made a limiting decision, our mistaken interpretation of what occurred redefined and distorted our experience of reality in that area of our life.

This explanation of the process we go through as children is not meant as a criticism or even to imply we made a mistake. This happens to all of us and is just how the human experience works. (The second part of this book addresses how to undistort the distortions of our limiting decisions.)

Common Limiting Decisions

There are many possible limiting decisions we might make in reaction to our early life experiences. Here are some of the most common ones I've come across:

- I am bad, not wanted, unlovable, stupid, not good enough, wrong, unacceptable, inadequate, a burden, a failure, worthless, powerless.
- I can't have what I really want.
- I don't deserve to be happy.

- I don't fit in.
- I'm on my own.
- There's no one I can count on.
- I deserve to be punished.
- I'm not going to survive.
- I'm defective.
- If I am who I am, I won't succeed.
- Those I'm dependent on are dependent on me.
- Men are more valuable (powerful, significant) than women.
- Men have the power in the world.
- Male power is dangerous.
- Women can only have power through men.
- Women are weak.
- Emotions make you weak.
- There is not enough.
- Having sex is immoral.
- Being angry is bad.
- Self-interest is wrong.
- Being selfless is virtuous.
- Life is about hardship and misery.
- Surviving takes constant struggle.
- The world is a dangerous place.
- The world (life) is out of control.
- People only care about themselves.
- People can't be trusted.

The Effect of Limiting Decisions on Our Relationships

Limiting decisions are usually made in the context of some form of relationship. For that reason (as we saw in the example of Mary), they can have a major effect on our relationships.

Here's another, more complete, example of this:

> Let's say you were seven years old, and you were with your older brother, John. He's someone you always looked up to and trusted. He gave you a plastic bag of marijuana. You didn't know what it was, but it looked to you like dried weeds. John told you to hide it in your room for safekeeping. He told you it was a secret surprise for your mother, so you shouldn't tell her about it. You were all happy, thinking John was trusting you with something important to do, and your mother would be pleased.
>
> Instead, when your mother cleaned your room, she found the bag and went into a meltdown—yelling and screaming at you as if you had wounded her. You felt bewildered and shocked. Throughout your whole life, you had trusted your brother and mother. In that moment, you no longer knew who or what you could trust, including yourself. As a result, you made the limiting decisions that you can't trust those you're dependent on, you can't trust yourself, and that you're bad.

(You might wonder if you couldn't have just gotten angry at your brother and told your mother what happened when she calmed down. In traumatic events in which we make limiting decisions, we can't mentally or emotionally remain present.

25

Because our limiting decisions have distorted the event's meaning to us, we can't respond rationally.)

As noted earlier, limiting decisions come in the form of generalized decisions, and the people who were the focus of those decisions represented categories of people to you. When you made your limiting decisions, how you perceived the nature of those categories of relationships became distorted.

In this example, your concept of the symbolic relationships your brother and mother represented to you shifted according to how you interpreted what happened in that moment. How you conceive of intimate relationships with women you're dependent on or with men and boys has now been distorted. As a result, you may have difficulty getting into intimate relationships or getting emotionally close to people.

How Can Something (Apparently) Outside Your Control Be Caused by Your Limiting Decisions?

Limiting decisions can cause you to behave in ways you are not aware of that can have a large effect on how others react to you. Since you would be unaware of the effect you are having, it would feel to you that their reaction to you was outside your control.

> For example, when a man named Bob drove on the freeway, he often encountered drivers acting out of road rage toward him. This appeared to him completely outside his control.
>
> As it turned out, Bob had a lot of anger in him. In therapy sessions, we cleared the limiting decisions that he's powerless and not worthy of respect that were at

the bottom of his anger. After that, he no longer encountered angry drivers when driving on the freeway. It is likely that his aggressive, angry behavior when driving (that he had been unconscious of) was what brought out this angry response from other drivers.

Limiting Decisions Can Affect the Choices You Make

Limiting decisions can also cause results that appear outside your control by affecting the choices you make.

We frequently make choices in our lives, many of which are subtle and unconscious. You choose the order you will do particular things in your day, where to focus your mind in any moment, what event to go to, and who to talk to or who not to.

Each choice can set off a chain of events orchestrated by your unconscious mind. You would probably be unaware that the results you experience originated from the choices you made.

Let's say two friends, Ted and Rita, left phone messages for you. Which friend do you call back first?

As it happens, some issues about your health have been on your mind. This affects your choice. You decide to call Rita back first, although you are not conscious of why. You talk with her about your health and decide to take the advice she gives you. This leads to further options and choices, all of which could have a large positive or negative effect on your well-being.

When you call Ted back, since you already talked with Rita about your health, your focus is no longer on your health. You talk with Ted about something else. Ted has some information related to your health issue that you never end up finding out about. If you had found out about it, it would have taken you down a different path.

The unconscious reason you called Rita back first was that you know what she is likely to say would reinforce what you already thought. You were afraid Ted might have a different idea. You were afraid to open your mind to something different because you tend to be swayed too easily by other people's opinions. You get swayed too easily because of your limiting decision that you can't trust your perceptions.

And so, your limiting decision that you can't trust your perceptions resulted in you making an unconscious choice that limited the options you allowed into your life.

Limiting Decisions Can Decrease Your Awareness of the Choices You Are Even Aware Of

Limiting decisions can limit the choices you are aware of (or pay attention to) to those that prove your limiting decisions are true.

Perhaps you have made the limiting decision that you are not good enough. As a result, you find yourself in jobs that don't require much skill, aren't fulfilling, don't pay well, and don't offer advancement.

Many of your unconscious choices limited your options and got you to this place—all fueled by believing you are not good enough. Say a friend told you about a class that was an opportunity to learn a higher level of skills. You never put it in your calendar, and you forgot about the class. Or, you procrastinated so long about taking the class that by the time you decided to act on it, it was no longer available. You may not even notice when these kinds of opportunities come up. Perhaps you unconsciously filter them out as not applying to you.

Limiting Decisions Are Never Caused by People or Circumstances Outside of You

The concept of limiting decisions is empowering as it brings you out of a victim perspective. It may seem to you that people and life circumstances outside of you caused your limiting decisions. And it's true, someone may have done some action toward you that resulted in you making a limiting decision. But limiting decisions are created on the basis of how *you interpreted* the meaning of something that occurred. They are not based on what someone actually did to you or by the pain someone or something caused you.

For example:

A tree branch falling and breaking your arm might physically hurt more than your mother slapping you and calling you stupid when you were two. However, if you interpreted your mother's actions as meaning that you are actually, inherently, a stupid person, it would cause a lot more damage than the tree branch falling on you. And it has the potential to last a lifetime. It's your interpretation of what happened that caused the lasting damage, not what your mother did.

Here's an example from a therapy session:

> Bonnie had a limiting decision that she is not wanted by the important men in her life. Under hypnosis, we discovered the origin of this decision took place when she was four years old. She made the limiting decision based on something she thought she heard her father say. But, when we examined the scene more closely, she realized what she heard came from a male voice on a TV show that happened to be on at that moment. It wasn't something her father had said at all.

CHAPTER THREE

The Substitute Persona

When you make limiting decisions about yourself in traumatic situations, (like all of us) you dissociate from your self and redefine how you perceive your self. As described in the previous chapter, you now experience this redefinition of your self as your real self. It has become a substitute for your real self. In the Life Is Designed to Work thought system, this is called a substitute persona.

You might think that several commonly used concepts are what I mean when I refer to the substitute persona. But those concepts come from a very different perspective.

One of them is the ego. We generally think of the ego as the aspect of the self that is aware of itself. We use having a strong or weak ego to describe how strong our sense of self is. This relates to our sense of self-worth. An egotistic person is generally defined as being arrogant or thinking too much of himself.

Other concepts that might be confused with the substitute persona are the psychological term sub-personality and the NLP use of the word "part." Both are generally defined as parts of us that separate from the self.

In addition, many of us refer to the "shadow" aspect of ourselves or others when we mean the part of ourselves we consider to be dark or negative.

In the Life Is Designed to Work thought system, the substitute persona replaces these concepts. Unlike these concepts, our substitute persona is not defined as a part of our self. It is a made-up self that only shows up in the areas of your life in which you have made limiting decisions.

Your substitute persona believes itself to be unlovable, a failure, stupid, not good enough, or whatever limiting decisions it has made. Its function is to hold in place the distorted reality created by its limiting decisions. Your substitute persona exists only as long as you hold in place your limiting decisions.

Here is an example of how a substitute persona is formed, based on the hypothetical scenario about you, your brother, and your mother I gave in the last chapter:

> In this scenario, when you believed your brother and acted on what he told you to do, you were a vulnerable, loving, trusting seven-year-old child. When you made the limiting decisions that you can't trust yourself and that you are bad, you turned against that vulnerable, trusting self (your real self). You blamed that self for the pain you were in. To the unconscious mind, that undistorted, vulnerable self is what destabilized you when the traumatic event occurred.
>
> As a result, you split off from that vulnerable, real self, shoving it down into your unconscious mind, separated from your conscious awareness. You then replaced it with your substitute persona. This persona helped you make sense of the traumatic experience. It is now who

32

you mistakenly experience yourself to be. (This process is all happening on an unconscious level.)

The Effect Our Substitute Persona Has on Our Relationships

Before the original event happened, you had the potential for a loving, close relationship with your brother and your mother. You also had the potential for receiving emotional nourishment and evolving yourself within your close relationships, in general.

When you made limiting decisions and began forming your substitute persona, you started distancing yourself from that potential. Now, instead of relating to others as a vulnerable, trusting little child and evolving yourself forward, you relate to others from your distorted, substitute persona who is stuck believing it can't trust those it's dependent on or itself, and that it is bad.

Every time you made another limiting decision, you were building an increasingly distorted persona with less potential for a fulfilling relationship with yourself as well as others.

(The potential in you for fulfilling relationships has nothing to do with whether those around you are emotionally available. In every situation we're in, there may be people who are emotionally available and those who aren't or people who can be trusted and those who can't. When you make a limiting decision, in the areas of your life affected by the limiting decision, you are unable to receive the gifts that are actually there for you regardless of what may or may not be wrong with the people around you.)

As mentioned previously, your substitute persona only exists in the areas of your life affected by the limiting decisions you have made. In areas of your life in which you haven't, you live from your real, undistorted self.

Our Substitute Persona Is Often How We Identity Ourselves

We can become very invested in our substitute persona as our identity, as who we experience ourselves to be. It generally is how we show up out in the world.

Let's say that as a small child, you made a limiting decision that you are a failure. This might result in you creating a persona that shows up as self-effacing, inadequate, and uncertain in how it relates out in the world. You (in the form of your substitute persona) are afraid to try anything you might fail in. This greatly limits your options and gets in the way of you moving forward in life. You are preventing yourself from ever succeeding.

Or, if you form an effective defense system in relation to the same limiting decision, your persona might have its heart sealed off and show up as an aggressive salesperson or top executive. You might plow forward in your career regardless of how it affects others and regardless of whether the work is meaningful for you.

This defended persona is how you feel like a success and how you get symbols of respect and power in your life. This gives you the illusion of getting some form of satisfaction and making progress.

But because you avoid finding out what is actually true, you block yourself from engaging in what truly matters to you. You are blocking yourself from truly becoming empowered and successful.

Emotional Defense Systems

Our substitute persona lives in the pain of our limiting decisions. As soon as we formed our persona, we started developing emotional defense systems to defend ourselves against that pain. Defense systems are emotional walls or attacks that protect us from the perceived source of pain. The perceived source is generally the people or situations that bring up that pain in you. In those situations, as a defense, we might be reactive, judgmental, controlling, or just plain unaware.

(The defenses we put up are happening on an unconscious level. We are usually not aware we are doing this.)

Once we form our defenses, two conflicting things are happening, mostly on an unconscious level: We try to defend ourselves from the pain of our limiting decisions while, at the same time, our unconscious minds try to maintain our stability by holding our limiting decisions in place. So we are holding what causes the pain in place while trying to get rid of the pain.

Pretty self-defeating, isn't it!?

Some of us develop effective defenses, while others of us don't. Those of us with less effective defenses live more in the pain of our limiting decisions. Life clearly is not working for us. We feel at the mercy of what we mistakenly believe to be true about ourselves or the world around us.

Having less effective defenses may seem to be a problem because we can't avoid our pain very well. But because we live in pain, we are usually more conscious of the actual problem we have, such as that we feel unlovable, bad, or a failure. For that reason, we are motivated to find actual solutions, such as seeking therapeutic help.

Those with more effective defenses are more able to avoid living in their pain. They are better at staying unconscious of what they falsely believe to be true about themselves. They are far less likely to seek any kind of solution or therapeutic help because they don't recognize there is a problem.

Narcissism is a good example of an effective defense system. Many people who use this defense are charismatic and do well in their careers. They can charm people into doing what they want. Their experience is that they are in control of the world around them.

Substitute personas that are well-defended focus on trying to prove the opposite of the limiting decisions they have made. Their purpose is to get by in the world in a way that compensates for, maneuvers around, avoids, or in some way is a denial of what they mistakenly decided was true about themselves.

They're trying to control reality rather than work with what is real and true because they believe what is real and true is against them. In other words, they believe the truth is that they are, for example, a failure, bad, or unlovable.

They try to control reality by trying to control how they are perceived. Their efforts go into, for example, being *perceived* as successful, good, or lovable. This is the point of their life, although they are not consciously aware of the actual purpose of what they are doing. It may just seem to them that this is the way people can be successful. They do this rather than trying to find an actual solution for their mistaken beliefs about themselves. Actual solutions would allow actual success and love to come into their lives.

For those of us with less effective defenses, it can feel as though we just can't defend ourselves against the pain. But the reason we don't defend ourselves well is not that we are ineffective or weak. The reason is often that we are more in contact with the essence of who we are (i.e., our real self). Therefore, compromising ourselves in the way those with effective defense systems do feels too painful. It's too much out of alignment with who we are.

Now to be clear, most of us with limiting decisions are defended to some degree. Most of us defend ourselves against feeling worthless, not good enough, bad, or whatever our limiting decisions are by trying to prove the opposite. It's really a matter of how invested we are in our defenses.

How Our Emotional Defenses Interact with Other People

The defenses of our substitute personas are often an accepted way of behaving in the world (depending on how subtle or extreme they are). In fact, calling attention to the emotional defenses of others is generally considered rude. As a result, we usually get away with acting them out on each other.

Manipulating people is one way our defenses commonly show up. The substitute personas of other people do it to us, and we do it to them. We all experience this happening, but we aren't usually conscious of what is actually happening or its purpose.

For example, in the case of Mary, since she has decided that men, in general, are dangerous, rather than actually being present to who a particular man is, she imposes on him her distorted perception of how men are.

As an emotional defense against "dangerous men," Mary (as her substitute persona) might manipulate men sexually. She might act in provocative ways toward them, be flirtatious, or wear seductive clothes. She does this in order to feel she has the control and is, therefore, safe.

Perhaps, in your own life experience, you have observed the substitute personas of women (and men) using the emotional defense of sexual manipulation.

As another example of an emotional defense, perhaps you know someone who often steers conversations in a way that proves that he is superior to others. He might unconsciously do this as a defense against feeling inferior.

Maybe you find yourself making everything a joke, especially when you're nervous, so you don't feel unacceptable. You may notice you do this but may feel unable to stop. You probably think this is just who you are.

Or maybe you unconsciously send subtle, nonverbal signals to other people to not notice you, or to keep their distance, or to not look at you directly. You may do this to avoid being rejected. You probably have no idea you are doing this. You may just be aware that you feel invisible. You don't realize you are doing something that causes people not to notice you, and that's why you feel invisible.

The Negative Impact Emotional Defense Systems Can Have on Our Lives

Our emotional defense systems can have a negative impact on our lives. Here is an example involving interactions in a work situation:

> Amy had a small business and was effective at getting things done on her own. When she had to delegate work to others, she had a much harder time.

Amy had a team of workers and felt frustrated with them. The work they did was frequently under par and took far too long to do. She often had to redo it or finish up jobs herself. She put a lot of effort into training and supporting her workers, but they didn't seem to improve. She was convinced that's just the way workers are.

Amy's limiting decision at the bottom of the situation was that if she depends on others, they will have control over her. This resulted in a defense system in which she avoided depending on anyone for anything. She always had to be in control.

As a result, those she hired tended to be weak people she could control so she wouldn't feel threatened. But the result was they didn't do a good job, couldn't make decisions, and couldn't work well on their own. Even those who were capable of making decisions were afraid to because of Amy's micromanaging.

As you can see, Amy's emotional defense system didn't help her in reality. It got in the way of her having productive, healthy relationships with her workers. This, in turn, undermined the success of her business.

The Impermanence of Our Emotional Defense Systems

For most people, emotional defense systems are not effective permanently. They take a lot of energy to hold in place. As we get older, our energy generally decreases, making it harder to keep them up.

In addition, defense systems can limit the possibilities in our life to what we can control. This can become a problem because what truly matters to you often requires you to expand beyond what's in your control.

What truly matters to you might require you to leave a comfortable, safe relationship that feels wrong for you; or it might mean taking a job you are very interested in but are afraid you won't be good enough to succeed in; or it might be admitting to someone you love how you really feel about him/her.

Eventually, what truly matters to you may become so strong, your self-imposed limitations become too painful to maintain. You can no longer maintain control over your defense systems. They then start breaking down, and you may not be able to defend yourself against the pain of your limiting decisions. You may not be able to defend yourself against feeling, for example, that you are a failure, not good enough, not lovable, or not safe.

You might start getting symptoms, such as difficulty sleeping, anxiety, depression, or dissatisfaction with your relationships and the way you have been living your life. Maybe you now notice a lack of meaning in your life, a lack of purpose. Or maybe you're in love with someone but feel frustrated with the relationship because you can't let down the walls to allow him/her in.

These kinds of feelings and symptoms generally show up when your real self is ready to move past the limitations of your defense systems.

This is the time to focus on and allow into your awareness what the limiting decisions are you have been defending yourself against. Becoming aware of them is the first step in moving toward a solution.

CHAPTER FOUR

What We Choose to Give Our Life Stability

The concept of a plumb line is useful in helping us understand what we need in order to have a stable source for our survival and well-being:

> A plumb line is a string or cord that is weighted on the bottom end. It is a basic carpentry tool used to align physical structures (such as a building) with gravity so they will be stable.

> Gravity is a physical force that the structure of our physical world depends on. The force of gravity pulls the plumb line straight down and, therefore, provides an accurate vertical orientation. If a building is aligned with that true vertical plumb line, it will be stable. If a building is oriented around a wall that is tilted, and, therefore, not aligned with gravity, the building won't be stable.

We generally orient ourselves around one or more sources outside ourselves that we believe will provide stability for our survival and well-being. They become our plumb lines.

Similar to the carpenter orienting his building around a plumb line, what we orient our lives around determines whether our life works or not. And, therefore, the plumb line you choose is crucially important. If your plumb line is not aligned with a true source (such as gravity is for a building), sooner or later, it will not be stable and will not support your survival and well-being.

Here are some common plumb lines many of us use to give ourselves a sense of stability in our lives:

A Person

Many of us orient our life around a person, such as a husband, a wife, or a teacher, as our plumb line.

Perhaps you know someone whose life revolves around her significant other. Many people rely on their significant other for their security, financial survival, sense of value, and/or well-being. Perhaps you recognize this in yourself. Or, perhaps, instead of a significant other, for you, that person is a best friend, an adult child, or a parent.

You might rely on that person for what you believe you can't handle. For example, you might rely on him to make decisions for you, or to take actions out in the world for you, or as your conscience. You might do this because you don't trust your own judgment, believe you can't take care of yourself, or are afraid the world is too much for you. Or perhaps you feel if you don't orient your life around this person, he will leave you.

(When this person is also using you as his plumb line that is a co-dependent relationship.)

When you orient your life around a person, you are actually orienting yourself around his perception of reality. To whatever degree his perception is distorted or disconnected from present-moment experience, you are leaning on the distortions and limitations through which he is defining his life.

In addition, other people aren't inside of your experience. Although they may have wisdom or experience to offer, they ultimately can't know the best choices for you. They are not what your survival, well-being, and stability can actually be based on.

In the long run, orienting your life around another person is limiting, disempowering, and, therefore, destabilizing.

Your Home

For most of us, our home is an important plumb line. It gives us a stable location to exist and build our life.

Our home gives us a sense of safety from the outside world. It is a buffer, enabling us to filter input from the world according to our needs and desires.

We generally feel some control over the environment inside our home, or at least we expect to have control over it, such as what our home looks like, how clean it is, and the music or noise level. We want it to be a stable reality for us, where we can know what to expect, as opposed to the environment out in the world.

If you are overly invested in using your home to create a stable reality you control, you're likely to feel disconnected from the larger world. You might do this if you feel unsafe in life, the world feels out of control to you, or you feel you don't belong or fit in the world.

Perhaps you know someone who is compulsive about keeping her home neat and clean. Dishes are never lying around, and nothing is out of order. Whenever she has had a hard or upsetting day, and her life feels out of control, she retreats to her home and vacuums every square inch of it even though it's already completely clean. She micromanages anyone who comes into her home, which results in few visitors.

Using her home as a plumb line in this way enables her to avoid dealing with whatever feels out of control in her life. But by avoiding what she needs to deal with, she is actually causing her life to be out of control.

Or, you may know someone with an opposite kind of personality. This person might have limiting decisions, such as there is not enough and he is not safe.

He might be a hoarder, saving everything in case he might need it. Piles of things build up on his living room floor, giving him less and less space to move around. He is embarrassed to invite anyone over because of this. But he keeps doing this because he feels safe and comfortable with all his things around him. They are almost like friends for him. He is creating an increasingly smaller world for himself, boxing himself into a corner.

These are examples of people trying to create a stable and safe reality by orienting themselves around what they believe they can control. But to do that, they have to greatly limit their lives, and the opportunities and options they have available to them.

Most of the ways we use our homes as our source of stability in the world are less extreme than these examples. Nonetheless, most of us would be upset if we lost the stability and sense of control over our survival needs and well-being that our home provides for us.

And that could happen because, as permanent as a home may seem, even if you own it, life has a way of reminding us that we are never really in control. Natural phenomena, such as fires and floods, are not uncommon, and life circumstances can change in unexpected ways.

Your Job or Business

For those of us who support ourselves, our job or business is a significant plumb line we orient our lives around. It provides financial stability for our survival and well-being—or at least it is meant to. It can also provide a stable environment we structure our time around.

If we work at an office outside of our home, we spend much of our day in a familiar environment that becomes like a second home. We come to rely on what we can expect during our time there.

For some of us (by choice or by necessity), our work occupies most of our time. This might result in neglecting our relationships and even our own well-being. Our work can become the focus of our whole life.

Regardless of the circumstances, work situations carry inherent risks. Businesses can fail, management can change, the economy can take a downturn, people can be laid off, and work environments can become unsustainable.

———

In the physical realm, gravity is a force defined by the laws of physics. It is connected to something inherently real and true. For that reason, orienting a physical structure around gravity provides fundamental stability for that structure.

In contrast, the examples given in this chapter (particular people, your home, or your job) are not inherently real and true. Therefore, orienting yourself around them does not provide a solid source of stability. (I'm not saying your job, home, and relationships aren't important. They are just not the basis for your underlying stability.)

What would be a plumb line that *is* in alignment with what is inherently real and true and that *can* give us real stability for our survival and well-being? And why do we choose limited, unstable sources instead?

CHAPTER FIVE

Separation from Our Source

Now let's look at a true source for a life that works and why we tend to rely on substitute sources instead. This requires shifting to a metaphysical perspective.

By metaphysical, I mean a larger perspective beyond our physical experience. I'm coming from the perspective that there is a larger, nonphysical source we are ultimately dependent on. I refer to It as Source. Perhaps you are accustomed to referring to It as God, The Divine, Holy Spirit, The Creator, The Universe, or Larger Truth. In this larger nonphysical perspective, Source is eternal and is the source of everything that has real existence.

This larger perspective includes the view that we each have a soul, and our soul is the essence of who we are. Our soul exists beyond our physical body. It existed before we were born and continues to exist after our body dies.

The Confusion about Where Our Source Is

Before we are born, we, as souls, feel connected to Source. But when we are born, it appears that few of us still feel connected to or even consciously remember the nonphysical Source we came from. For that reason, few of us grow up having an internal experience of Source without a significant amount of intention and focus.

Once we are born, our environment and world are radically different from the nonphysical world we came from. The basic requirement in this new environment is physical survival. Keeping our physical body alive—fed, clothed, and safe—is a daily priority.

We now view the physical world (such as our parents and the physical environment around us) as our bottom-line source for providing what we need.

We depend on our parents to define reality for us. We take what they say or think as representing the truth about us and the way life inherently is. As a result, many of the limiting decisions we make are formed because of how they act or what they say.

For instance, your parents may say or do unevolved things, such as telling you that you are stupid or worthless, or blaming you for their unhappiness, or that you can't trust anyone outside of the family. Or they might act in ways that give you the idea that life is about struggle or that status is what gives you value. We, as children, then take these distorted ideas or perceptions as truth and make limiting decisions about ourselves and the world as a result.

This happens because we have forgotten who we are, where we came from, and what we are really dependent on. We have

50

forgotten the larger context we all, including our parents, are a part of.

So we have gone from knowing our real source is a nonphysical Source—to being born into this physical experience and firmly believing our sources are our parents and the physical world around us.

Our Investment in Control

In primitive times, it appears humans had little control. Anything could happen. We could be attacked at any time by wild animals or enemy tribes. It appears we had little or no understanding about how to protect ourselves from hurricanes, droughts, or famines.

As we gained more consciousness, we began to understand how we could bring more order and security into our lives. We gained more understanding about the cycles of nature and planned accordingly. We created more effective shelters to protect us from the elements and wild animals. We made tools and organized hunting parties and other divisions of work.

As we became more civilized, cooperation between people became important for our survival and well-being. We made agreements and pacts (such as between warring parties or within communities) about behavior and what we could expect from each other, according to what mattered to each party. That gave us more of a sense of control over our survival, security, and well-being. There was increasingly more order in life.

The human concept of progress largely has to do with becoming more in control of our environment. It has to do with things working smoothly, as expected, in a way that makes us feel the way we want to. It makes us feel safe. It makes us feel good about ourselves. It makes us feel in control of our lives and as though we can make life be what we choose to make it.

We have become invested in perceiving ourselves as having control over our lives as our main and daily source of survival, well-being, and stability.

Civilization in developed countries has advanced to the point where we have a lot of power and control in our lives. We can easily turn lights on or off, heat our homes to whatever temperature we desire, communicate with each other across the world, access huge amounts of information at our convenience, and fly across the globe. We expect businesses to cater to our needs and desires. We complain when we don't have good customer service. We expect to be in control of our lives to a large degree.

Even though a significant number of us believe that some version of God or Divinity is in control of our lives, in practice, most of us believe we humans have the control or ought to have the control. When we have difficulties in life, what we rely on as our bottom-line defense is our own control or some human source out in the world that we can access.

Examples of these human sources (some of which I described in the previous chapter) are our parents for physical and financial support; our husband or wife, who supports us physically and emotionally; our job that gives us financial security; our doctors or healthcare providers to help us when we're sick; local and federal governments that provide services we depend on; and the police who keep dangerous people from harming us.

Our Power Struggle against Source

We trust our own control rather than Source because, since Source is not physical, we don't totally believe It exists. In addition, we feel powerless over affecting Source to get what we want. We much prefer our own control.

For that reason, the realization we are actually dependent on a larger, nonphysical Source is not something most of us acknowledge unless we get into an overwhelming crisis (such as a catastrophic illness or losing our job or home). We usually only acknowledge we are dependent on Source when we are desperate and feel hopeless about there being any solution within human control.

CHAPTER SIX

The Alternate Reality We Live In

Throughout our lifetimes, we experience opportunities to expand beyond where we are in order to evolve ourselves forward. In childhood, this sometimes happens during overwhelming, traumatic, or intense experiences that shatter how we had been experiencing what was real. These traumatic experiences cause us to lose the stable sense of reality we had been living in. (This is the type of experience described in Chapter Two, in which most of us made limiting decisions.)

When this happens, if we can expand our awareness beyond our immediate situation and beyond our shattered experience of what is real, we can become aware of a larger perspective of what is happening in that moment. This larger perspective would give us a more evolved understanding of what is happening and a more stable experience of reality than what has just been shattered.

For example, if Mary (in Chapter Two) had been able to expand her awareness and recognize the larger environment she was actually living in beyond what her father encompassed, she might have noticed that not all men were like her father. This might have enabled her to notice that there was something seriously wrong with her father. She would, therefore, not have used her father's behavior to form her definition of the nature of men. From this larger perspective, she might also have realized that her father reacting as though she was bad couldn't define who she was.

Mary's experience of reality would have then expanded and evolved, giving her a more real source of stability. As a result, she would not have made the limiting decisions.

However, (as I described in the previous chapter) many, if not most of us, live our lives separated from consciousness of Source. For that reason, when traumatic experiences occurred in childhood, we were not aware there was a larger, positive source beyond our immediate environment.

As a result, our perspective of reality was confined to and defined by a much more limited and much less true source. That limited source usually was whoever had power over us or who we were dependent on. (In Mary's case, that was her father.)

From this limited and distorted perspective, we made limiting decisions to regain a stable sense of reality.

Limiting Decisions—the Foundation for Our Substitute World

Chapter Two explained that our model of reality is based on an unconscious process of filtering in some of the information that bombards our senses every moment. The point of taking in information is to know what is in our environment. We're looking for what is actually there so we can know how to function in our world.

But in the areas of our lives in which we made our limiting decisions, what we choose to filter in is no longer motivated by finding out what is actually there. What we choose to filter in is based on imposing our limiting decisions onto our experience of reality and trying to prove our limiting decisions are what is real and true.

As a result, in these areas of our lives, we create a model of reality for ourselves that is separate from the truth of what is there. It is separate from Source. This model of reality is a stand-in for what is real and true. In the Life Is Designed to Work thought system, this model of reality is called a "substitute world."

In the areas in our life affected by our limiting decisions, the stability of our perception of reality depends on our ability to uphold this substitute world. Until we're ready to expand ourselves and evolve forward, it is the only form of stability we have available.

Our Substitute World

Our substitute world is an inner experience in which the limiting decisions we have made control how we experience ourselves and others. It's like being stuck in a room in our mind that is our own personal hell. It's a whole, distorted reality system.

In our substitute world, we (in the form of our substitute persona) might experience ourselves as unlovable, not worthy of respect, and/or powerless. We might experience others as dangerous, irresponsible, and/or not trustworthy. Our substitute persona is in charge of maintaining this experience and stands vigil to make sure nothing shakes its stability.

After you make a limiting decision, (in the areas of your life affected by that limiting decision) you are living your life as a substitute persona (rather than your real self). The experience of your substitute persona and of being in your substitute world is the same because you are in your substitute persona when you are in your substitute world. They are a part of the same distorted reality system.

To maintain this experience, we tend to bring into our lives those who have the same or similar negative behavior patterns as those in the original traumatic events (or their behavior can be interpreted in that way).

We project the pain of our limiting decisions onto these people, believing they are the sources of our pain. We experience them as making us feel unloved, unsafe, disrespected, powerless, and so on. We experience them as though they were the same people we made our limiting decisions in relation to with the same kind of power over us.

We keep replaying the same loop in which the same people cause the same kinds of painful things to keep happening to us that were happening in that original event.

Our World of Stories

One way we hold our substitute world in place is by telling ourselves and others stories that describe what we believe is happening in our substitute world. These stories are usually some form of blaming others for our pain. Our stories describe our subjective interpretations of other people's motives and actions as if our interpretations are objective truth.

We're not interested in actual truth because that would undermine our limiting decisions and our substitute world. We are invested in proving these stories are true because they support the reality we feel dependent upon for our stability.

When we get into conflicts with others, it's usually because each of us is trying to prove our own story is true and the other person's story is wrong.

A conflict that occurred between a couple, Amanda and Andrew, is a good example:

Amanda's story is that Andrew dismissed her when she gave her opinion about an event reported in the news. In doing so, he made her feel put down and humiliated, something he regularly does to her.

Andrew's story is that Amanda isn't capable of understanding the issues involved and so wasting his time discussing the event with her is an imposition on him.

When this conflict happened, Amanda was triggered by the limiting decision that she is inadequate. Andrew was triggered by the limiting decision that women are incapable of functioning out in the world, which leaves the whole burden on men.

(By "triggered" I mean when intense, upsetting emotions, such as anger or fear, are activated in you. This is caused by the pain of a limiting decision being brought to the surface of your awareness.)

They both tend to defend themselves against the pain of their limiting decisions with certain negative behaviors they feel justified in doing. For example:

Amanda doesn't pay close attention to something happening in the news before she gives an opinion. She does this because putting out that effort would bring up her pain of believing she's too inadequate to understand it.

Andrew defends himself against his pain by avoiding having conversations with Amanda about anything substantial. And when he does have them, he doesn't really listen to her. This reinforces Amanda's feeling that she's not adequate.

Neither Amanda nor Andrew wants to find out what is actually true. They are invested in proving their stories that their painful feelings are being caused by the other.

Amanda does not want to admit that feeling inadequate is something she experiences in other circumstances besides with Andrew. She doesn't want to admit that feeling that way originates from inside of her and is a part of her painful inner world.

She does not want to be aware of what her behavior was that might have contributed to the conflict between them. That is because that awareness would not be a part of her substitute world where she perceives herself made to feel inadequate by the people around her, through no fault of her own.

Amanda is invested in coming out of this interaction with Andrew feeling justified in her response to him. She is holding in place a substitute world story she is familiar with. It is a story that holds in place conflict between them.

Andrew is doing something similar in relation to Amanda. Both are holding in place a painful distortion of reality that keeps repeating itself. It is a conflict-filled perception that reinforces both of their substitute worlds and results in neither finding happiness or fulfillment with each other.

Our Defended Substitute Worlds

When our substitute personas develop emotional defense systems to protect us from the pain of our limiting decisions, they also start developing defended substitute worlds to support those defenses. These defended substitute worlds exist outside us.

The environments we use as defended substitute worlds can be in the form of actual structures or situations in the world. Organizations and social structures (such as businesses, political groups, governments, religious organizations, clubs, and families) often are used for this purpose. These structures hold in place an agreed-upon way to experience reality that supports the views of whoever controls them.

Organizations are sometimes set up for the purpose of attracting those who resonate with the particular substitute reality being held in place, such as exclusive clubs, hate groups, or political alliances.

Substitute worlds can also come in the form of a more personal, generalized experience. They can be made up of the people and situations that comprise our day-to-day life.

In our defended substitute worlds, we attach the same symbolic meanings to the environments around us as our original traumatic environments represented to us (such as an intimate relationship situation, a family environment, home, a place where friends gather, an environment where people have power or authority over others, an environment with the potential of power and success out in the world, or a place where people either do or don't fit in). And then we try to position ourselves

61

to control those symbolic environments, rather than being at their mercy as we were in the original traumatic situation.

It is in our defended substitute worlds that we (in the form of our defended substitute personas) find ways to compensate for, skirt around, or otherwise give the opposite impression to ourselves and to those who populate our world from what we mistakenly believed to be true and real when we made our limiting decisions.

For instance, if you have the limiting decision that you are inferior, in your defended substitute world you might try to prove you are superior. You might do that by manipulating, intimidating, or otherwise pressuring those who populate your world into upholding your story that you are superior.

As long as we succeed in defending ourselves against what we mistakenly believe to be true, we are not aware of the painful substitute world we actually live in.

In contrast, with a less defended substitute persona in a less defended substitute world, you might find yourself constantly struggling to succeed in life. You would feel like a loser, just barely making it through the day.

The Symbolic Meanings We Give to People and Situations in Our Defended Substitute Worlds

As I described previously, when we made our limiting decisions, the significant people and circumstances involved in those situations represented symbolic categories to us. The people and circumstances in our substitute worlds represent those same symbolic meanings for us.

Here's an example of this in a substitute world based on a general environment:

Let's say you are a young boy around twelve years old and your father died recently. Your mother, having to support the family by herself, can no longer afford the family's suburban home. She moves the family to a small house in the city to save on expenses.

At first, you like living in the city because there are many people from different cultures and backgrounds. You see boys rapping on the street corners, and there are lots of ethnic food places around. It feels as though you are right in the middle of life.

One night, you wake up when you hear sounds coming from somewhere in the house. You go to see what is happening. A man rushes at you and roughly knocks you down, causing you to gash your head on the dining room table. You think he might have a gun. He then runs out of the house.

In a state of trauma and shock, you make the limiting decisions that the world is a dangerous place and that you are powerless. You now experience the world around you as painful and dangerous. In it, you impose symbolic meanings onto the real people and circumstances that you believe could impact your safety and that of your family. The meanings you impose are in the form of categories, such as dangerous man, dangerous place, or enemy.

Without being conscious you are doing it, you have made up a defended substitute world that conforms to the reality experience you now believe to be true. Instead of participating in actual reality, to a large degree you are now living in this substitute world reality, which you project onto the environment around you.

As a result, you start withdrawing from life. You stay home as much as possible, making sure the doors are locked. And you stop making new friends.

You are now living in relation to symbols you believe you can have some control over—even if the control is simply avoiding those to whom you have given symbolic meanings. In that area of your life, you are now living in relationship to concepts in your head rather than what is actually happening outside yourself. What you conceive of as self-interest becomes more about the symbolism than about anything real.

Your goal becomes to distance yourself from the people in the neighborhood who symbolize danger to you and trigger that powerless feeling. You do that rather than learn to live in this cultural diversity and become empowered in reality.

This results in you, to a large extent, no longer being in present-moment experience in relation to survival. You won't be aware of actual danger unless it comes in a particular kind of symbolic form, such as from a heavy-set blond man (because the man who attacked you was heavy-set and blond). And you may react as if you are in danger in situations that are not actually dangerous. For example, you might start reacting as if your kind, heavy-set, blond, male neighbor is dangerous. Your neighbor has now become a symbol to you rather than a real person.

Because you have isolated yourself from experiencing and learning about the diverse world around you, you will not be very effective in learning how to interact with that world. You have now moved from living in direct relationship with other cultures to having distanced yourself from the actual reality of that diverse world. You are living in relation to symbols representing it.

In our substitute worlds, we relate to symbols rather than what is actually real, concepts rather than present-moment experience. We are just symbols to each other.

Substitute Desires

An important part of our defended substitute world realities are our substitute desires.

In the areas of our life in which we made our limiting decisions, we unconsciously block receiving what we need or desire. As a result of believing we are unlovable or not worthy of respect (or whatever the limiting decision is), we don't believe anyone would love or respect us. We are, therefore, not open to receiving love or respect.

Since you now believe you can't have those needs and desires, your substitute persona develops symbolic substitutes. It gives symbolic meanings to food, objects, people, people's behaviors, or situations in your life.

For instance, if you made the limiting decision you are not lovable, eating comfort food might symbolize being loved. If you made the limiting decision you are powerless, getting your significant other to do what you tell her to do might symbolize that you are powerful. In this thought system, these are called substitute desires.

In our defended substitute worlds, symbols of what we desire and need replace what we actually desire and need (but believe we can't have).

Most of us find ourselves going toward substitute desires to some degree.

Using Our Defended Substitute Worlds to Receive Our Substitute Desires

Being able to receive substitute desires is the substitute persona's idea of gaining mastery in life. The substitute persona uses its defended substitute worlds to gain its substitute desires.

For example:

> A man named Larry has the limiting decision that he isn't worthy of respect, so he doesn't respect himself. As a defense, he regularly lies to avoid taking responsibility for mistakes he makes. This results in family members not taking what he says seriously and not respecting him.
>
> Not realizing that his own behavior is the source of his family not respecting him, Larry defends himself against feeling disrespected by requiring strict obedience from his children. If they disobey him, he physically and emotionally abuses them, so they won't do it again.
>
> For Larry, receiving strict obedience from his children is a substitute desire that symbolizes being respected. He might set up his whole household as a substitute world that he can control, where everything has to be the way he wants it, and no one disobeys him. This gives him a sense of mastery over his life.
>
> But the truth is, in the commonly shared world (as opposed to his defended substitute world experience), when Larry acts this way, he achieves the opposite of what he's trying to do. He is eliciting even more disrespect from his wife and his children.

Here's an example of a different kind of defended substitute world set up to receive substitute desires and the result of living in it:

Adam, who has the limiting decision that he is a failure, owns a software company. He struggled with getting it off the ground for many years. Each time he failed, the pain of his limiting decision that he is a failure came to the surface. This resulted in him feeling even more like a failure. He thought it was the soft, feeling part of himself that was causing him to fail.

As a result, he started cutting off that vulnerable, heart-connected part of himself and started building a defended persona. When he did that, he found he could make cutthroat decisions and gain a lot of power in his business. His business had become a defended substitute world.

Adam attracted business partners and employees whose own substitute personas interlocked with his to uphold his defended substitute world. Together they built a business empire that had a lot of perceived power in the world. It brought him the status and material rewards he desired.

The rewards he received were substitute desires that symbolized success to him. Rather than basing his business on what was truly interesting or significant to him, he developed software based on how high-end it was and how much prestige it would bring. Despite these symbols of success, he had a vague, empty feeling inside.

For years, Adam, who was married, had felt driven to have secret affairs with younger women in order to satisfy this empty feeling. When he was about fifty-five, his wife divorced him because he was never home, and when he was, he was not emotionally present. And as a final straw, she found out about his latest affair.

The divorce jolted Adam into a realization that all of the work and effort he had put into building his business and lifestyle (that had made him feel so successful) had not resulted in bringing into his life anything truly meaningful. It had not given him anything that would make his life worth living. He felt suicidal because he suddenly realized he had lost everything. He had no idea how to move toward a life that would truly work for him.

The example of Adam is a well-known human theme that many movies have portrayed. It is sometimes referred to as a midlife crisis.

It illustrates the huge amount of effort and investment many people spend to build up their defended substitute world as if that will finally get them what they want. But since it is a substitute world, it only provides substitute desires—the opposite of true self-interest. When this world is revealed to be one of unfulfillment and pain, it can feel devastating.

Of course, this kind of crisis is not limited to midlife and certainly doesn't only happen to men. But it often happens in midlife because our mortality can become more real to us then. Whether or not our lives are going in a meaningful and fulfilling direction becomes a greater priority.

An Overview Perspective

In the areas of our life where we have not made limiting decisions, we have access to an undistorted experience of what is real. But, as a result of the limiting decisions we have made, most of us are living in the distortion of our substitute worlds to some extent.

Our defended substitute worlds are set up as substitute reality systems. They become the plumb lines around which our lives are oriented. We believe our substitute desires are what we need and want. And we believe our substitute persona is who we really are.

We don't realize that in upholding our substitute worlds, we are holding in place unstable, substitute realities that are against our well-being.

The substitute persona (and its world) is disconnected from whatever is not distorted by its limiting decisions. The substitute persona believes present-moment experience, truth, and real sources of love and well-being are its enemy. That is because anything it truly desires, or anything that really matters to it, feels either dangerous and/or something it can't have.

This holds in place a backward perception of reality. Instead of going toward real solutions, the substitute persona goes in the opposite direction, depending on substitutes and symbols to convince itself that it's getting or achieving something.

There is often an unspoken agreement between individuals and between aligned groups of people to support each other's substitute personas and worlds. This is how much of society gets along. However, individuals, groups of people, and nations also often have major conflicts based on power struggles between their conflicting substitute-world realities. A case could be made that that is the basis for most wars.

Noticing Your Substitute-World Experience Being Triggered

You may not be consciously aware that you even have limiting decisions and the resulting distortions if you have defended enough substitute worlds. You can be living in a made-up, substitute world without realizing it. It's only when something triggers us and our emotions feel out of control or disconnected from reality that we have some idea we are living in a distorted experience.

When we get triggered, this generally means something has broken through our sense of control over our defended substitute world. This leaves us experiencing the pain of our vulnerable, inner substitute world. We feel rejected, unloved, stupid, or whatever the limiting decisions are that have been triggered. And we experience the people and situations around us as causing our painful feelings.

Awareness is the first step in freeing yourself from this dis-empowering, painful distortion of reality.

Here's an exercise in noticing your painful, inner substitute-world experience being triggered:

▶ <u>Remember a situation in your life when you were triggered.</u>

For example:

Perhaps you come home from a hard day of work or some other experience that took a lot out of you.

You are looking forward to relaxing. You walk into your house and become aware of something that is upsetting to you.

Perhaps someone has left a sink full of dirty dishes; maybe you check your answering machine and an important work-related message you were supposed to get isn't there, or maybe your child hasn't come home yet, and you don't know where he is.

▶ If a limiting decision has been triggered in you by this situation, your painful, inner substitute world experience will emerge.

For example:

If the limiting decision "your needs don't matter" got triggered, you might experience the reality you are living in as populated by people who don't care about how you feel. This is the perception of reality you generally believe to be true, but it is usually unconscious. When something like the dirty dishes left in the sink happens, it brings this painful perception to the surface and serves as proof to you that this perception of reality is true.

Or, if the limiting decision "you're not valuable" came up, you might experience your reality as populated by people who don't value you. For instance, perhaps you thought your boss didn't value you enough to get back to you with that message.

Or, if the limiting decision that "the world is a dangerous place" got triggered, you might interpret the reality you are now living in as populated by dangerous people (who might harm your child).

(Now this holds true even though the people in your life likely have their own limiting decisions and distortions, and they are functioning from their own emotional defense systems. In other words, they may actually act as though you don't matter or act dangerously. The issue is still whether your response to them is a triggered response or not.

Remember, your unconscious mind is set up to prove your limiting decisions are true. So if someone does something that supports your limiting decision (such as being disrespectful or harmful), your unconscious mind will grab that opportunity to prove your limiting decision is true rather than find an actual solution.

In a distorted state, it is difficult to be objective about what is actually true about the other person. It is, therefore, difficult to find a positive solution to the situation.)

▶ **Your triggered response will cause you to feel intense emotions way beyond what is objectively happening.**

As a result, you may find yourself acting in ways that feel out of control or that don't feel like your usual self. *This is your substitute persona.*

▶ **To dull the pain of your triggered emotions, you may find yourself doing things that feel good in the moment but aren't actually good for you.** They don't actually help the situation you are in.

For example, maybe you distract yourself by watching TV, even though there are some immediate things you ought to do. Or maybe you start obsessively cleaning your house. Or maybe you eat a big bowl of chocolate ice cream. *These are substitute desires.*

Fortunately, you don't have to stay stuck in your triggered responses. The next chapter will teach a process for getting you out of a triggered state. This will help you get out of your substitute world.

PART TWO

SHIFTING FROM THE SUBSTITUTE TO THE REAL WORLD

CHAPTER SEVEN

Defusing Your Emotional Triggers

N ow we'll switch from understanding what the problem is to finding your way through it.

In this chapter, you'll learn a practical tool called the Defuse Your Emotional Triggers Process. It will help you shift out of your substitute world in your everyday life.

I began developing this process many years ago when I was in a relationship I often felt triggered by. I *really* wanted to give him a piece of my mind—and sometimes did. But knowing that wasn't helpful to me or to him, I decided to sit on myself and not contact him until I could take responsibility for my emotions. In that context, this process was born.

Being triggered by our limiting decisions can cause us to have a major shift in our emotional state. Perhaps you start out in a good, or at least neutral, mood—and then you're triggered by something that happens, and you shift, sometimes radically, into a negative emotional state.

Perhaps you get triggered by your husband, your wife, your child, your parent, your boss, or your employee. Maybe you get upset because you feel he is not taking you seriously or is not respecting you. Or perhaps you feel she is being irresponsible. Or maybe you feel he is misusing his power over you.

Maybe you can't have a simple conversation with your significant other without it escalating into an argument and one of you walking off. It may often feel he is making life impossible for you, and why doesn't he just do things differently.

You may find yourself consumed with thoughts about the person or situation that keep going round and round in your mind, perhaps building to increasingly intense feelings. Or maybe these thoughts and emotions just keep leaking into your mind when you need to be focusing on something else.

When these kinds of things happen, we generally feel that people and circumstances in our lives are causing us to feel that we are bad, or not valuable, or inadequate, or whatever it is, according to the limiting decision that has been triggered.

However, he or she didn't actually cause that pain you are feeling. Even if the person is acting in a dysfunctional way, the only thing she/he has actually done to you (and usually not on purpose) is trigger the pain of the limiting decision that was already inside you.

Maybe he questioned a decision you made that triggered your limiting decision that you're not good enough, or maybe she didn't follow through on something she promised she would do, which triggered your limiting decision that those you're dependent on are irresponsible.

As a result of her triggering your limiting decision, you experience that person as the enemy, threatening your sense of well-being. She/he has become a symbol to you (such as irresponsible woman, mean man, or stupid person) rather than who she really is. She has become a chess player in your substitute world.

The process you're about to learn shows you how to move out of that disempowered state (your substitute world)—where you believe the other person is the source of your painful feelings—and back into your emotional center where you can experience well-being and empowerment.

As noted in the previous chapter, we often live in our substitute world, whether or not we are in an actively triggered state. It is what structures our experience in the areas of our life distorted by our limiting decisions. When we are not in a triggered state, we are generally unaware we live in this distorted state.

But when our limiting decisions are triggered, we feel the uncomfortable feelings associated with them. This gives us the opportunity to become aware that we're in our substitute world so we can do something about it.

This is when the Defuse Your Emotional Triggers Process is helpful. Its purpose is to get you out of a state of unconscious, subjective reaction where you are stuck in your substitute world.

This enables you to take responsibility for your painful experience as coming from inside yourself. It guides you into becoming aware of how you are creating that experience in order to defuse it.

Knowing how to get yourself out of a triggered state is a big step in shifting out of your substitute world. You can then more easily come into the present moment with yourself and other people from a place of resourcefulness and empowerment.

And now let's begin:

The Defuse Your Emotional Triggers Process

~ Recall an event that happened to you recently that is still a trigger for you:

> Perhaps it was a conflict you had with your significant other, your child, or your boss. Or perhaps a clerk in a store behaved in a way you found upsetting.

> You'll be using this event and the emotional triggers it brings up in you to learn this process.

~ You'll need a notebook or some other means of note-taking.

▶ STEP 1. RECOGNIZE THE TRIGGER

Recognize you are in an emotionally triggered state:

This is the most important step and is the first step in becoming conscious. Without your conscious mind being aware you are triggered; your unconscious mind has free rein to continue down a triggered path. The rest of the process would be impossible to do.

> When an emotional trigger gets set off, many people have a sort of sick, rotten, familiar feeling in the pit of their stomach. Or, you might feel angry, scared, agitated, frustrated, hot, rigid, or disconnected.

> ~ Allow yourself to become fully conscious of what your triggered feeling feels like.

(The next two steps are optional. They are sometimes helpful when the triggered emotion is so strong it's hard to follow a rational process. In that case, it is necessary to dissipate the emotion before continuing.)

▶ STEP 2. (OPTIONAL) RELEASE THE EMOTION

Express the triggered emotion you are feeling (usually anger or grief):

~ If the emotion is anger, find a private place or muffle your voice in a pillow and release your emotions at full volume. Express it as pure emotion, such as: "I am ANGRY!!!" And/or punch something—whatever works best for you to release the emotion.

It is important that you don't direct angry expressions toward the person who triggered it. If you do, you are dumping your emotions on him or her. This is an attack on that person and leads to further unconsciousness rather than consciousness.

~ If the emotion is grief and you feel like crying, let the emotion out, only long enough to release the intensity.

It's important not to dwell on the triggered emotions. As you release the emotions, they will become less intense, enabling you to move beyond your immediate volatile response.

▶ STEP 3. (OPTIONAL) OBJECTIFY THE EMOTION

Objectify your triggered emotion by describing how it feels:

Objectifying your triggered emotion helps you get out of a subjective state, where you experience the emotion as having power over you. It can calm you down.

~ Notice where the emotion is located in your body.

81

Perhaps it is in your stomach, or in your chest, or in your throat.

~ Recognize that it is just a pattern of energy.

~ Notice what the energy feels like.

Is it hot or burning? Is it cold and rigid? Is it slow and heavy? Is it racing and frazzled?

~ Imagine moving the energy pattern around, perhaps moving it an inch upward or downward or sideways.

(You might find it helpful to write down your responses to the next steps.)

▶ STEP 4. GET CLEAR WHAT THE STORY IS

Get clear what the story is you are telling yourself about the cause of your emotional response:

When you are in conflict with someone, you usually tell yourself some kind of story, representing your version of what happened (such as what Amanda and Andrew were doing in the last chapter). The story is generally in the form of blaming someone for something he did or didn't do that brought up pain in you.

Like Amanda and Andrew, we are usually invested in proving our stories are true. That is because, as you might recall from the last chapter, our stories are what uphold our substitute worlds.

(Now, you may be aware that blaming someone or something for the pain you are in is not the most conscious thing to do. Because of this, you might feel resistant to framing your experience in the form of blame. I'm asking you to put aside that resistance, if you have it, during this process.

Your conscious mind may know better than to blame someone, but your unconscious mind certainly does not. And since we are in the process of getting conscious about what your unconscious mind is doing, we have to look at it square in the face.)

~ Notice what you are saying to yourself in its unedited form.

Perhaps you are saying:

"My daughter is selfish. She doesn't care about me, even though I've sacrificed so much for her. Yesterday she didn't invite me when she went out to lunch, even though she knew I was lonely because her father is out-of-town. She only includes me when she wants something from me."

Or, "My boss makes me feel stupid. He keeps telling me to do jobs I haven't been trained for. He doesn't explain to me the objective of the jobs. Then he criticizes me for getting it wrong."

Or, "My husband doesn't respect me. Whenever we go out, he doesn't ask me what I'd like to do or even ask for my opinion about what we do. When I make a suggestion, he puts it down."

~ Go ahead and write your story down. Feel your investment in proving it is true.

▶ STEP 5. OBSERVE THE NEXT PROGRESSIONS

Observe what the next progressions are of the story that is going on in your mind:

For most people, it goes from specific to larger and larger generalizations.

For example, the story might be, "My husband doesn't respect me." Then it might progress to, "He'll never respect me, no matter what I do." Then it might be, "I'll never have a happy life with anyone." And then, "I'll always be isolated and lonely."

> Becoming conscious of the progressions of your story gives you a more realistic perspective on it. You can observe your progressions getting less rational as your story expands into larger generalizations.

~ If your story goes through these kinds of progressions, go ahead and write down what the progressions are.

▶ STEP 6. RECOGNIZE YOUR VULNERABLE FEELING

**Bring your awareness inside yourself and become aware of the vulnerable feeling your story brings up:**

(If you are feeling angry, look for the vulnerable feeling underneath the anger.)

~ Experience the feeling separately from the story you have attached to it. Separate the feeling from the person you have projected it onto. Focus in on just yourself and notice your own feeling inside.

> Perhaps you are feeling insignificant, or stupid, or wrong, or powerless.

> You might feel resistance to being aware of what you are feeling. That's because you're coming in direct contact with the limiting decision. The whole purpose of projecting the pain of your limiting decision onto a person or situation outside of yourself is to try to get rid of the pain. (As, hopefully, you know by now, this

doesn't solve anything.) What we're doing in this process is in direct opposition to that defense mechanism.

The fear of those painful feelings causes you to avoid coming into the present moment with yourself and with other people. And avoiding the present moment prevents you from finding out that those feelings *are not based on truth*. It is safe to allow this painful awareness in and this process works because limiting decisions are never true.

In allowing this awareness in, you're moving your focus from outside yourself to inside yourself, where the real source of your pain is. You can only find the solution to your pain if you address it where its real source actually is.

~ So, go ahead and let yourself feel your painful, vulnerable emotions and write them down. Perhaps you feel worthless, stupid, powerless, bad, or unlovable.

These are just triggered emotions, and triggered emotions don't represent reality.

▶ STEP 7. ACKNOWLEDGE YOUR BELIEF

Get conscious of the belief you have about yourself that is causing the painful feeling at the root of the story:

~ Focus in on the vulnerable feeling you have just accessed and recognize it as your own belief about yourself rather than something someone else made you feel. That belief is that you are worthless, stupid, powerless, bad, unlovable, or whatever the painful emotion is.

It might be helpful, here, to become aware of the difference between what your conscious mind thinks and what your unconscious mind believes. Your conscious mind might not logically think you are worthless, but your unconscious mind is not based on logic.

When you find the belief that brings up the intense emotional feeling at the heart of your story, you have pinpointed what your limiting decision is. *It is important to get clear what the limiting decision is, even though it feels painful, because this allows you to be directly conscious of what you mistakenly believe so you can find out it is not true.*

▶ STEP 8. SAY "I'M TELLING MYSELF"

<u>Reframe how you are experiencing the painful emotion by saying, "I'm telling myself that [the limiting decision]":</u>

You are now moving from feeling controlled by the triggered emotion, as if that is reality, to understanding what the reality of this experience actually is. It is a mistaken decision you made about yourself on an unconscious level. It is totally made up by you, and you have been unconsciously holding it in place.

To effectively do this process, it is important to remember that after your limiting decision was originally made, your unconscious mind was then invested in proving that it was true.

You are now catching your unconscious mind in the very act of doing this.

~ To become conscious of what you are doing, acknowledge it by saying, "*I am telling myself that* [and then say the limiting decision]."

That would come out, for example, as, "*I am telling myself that I'm insignificant,*" or "*I am telling myself that I have no value.*"

In this way, your conscious mind is becoming conscious of what your unconscious mind is doing.

▶ STEP 9. FURTHER REFRAME USING "REALLY GOOD EXCUSE"

Further reframe how you are experiencing the limiting decision by saying, "All this experience is, is just a really good excuse for my unconscious mind to prove the belief (that I already had) that [whatever the limiting decision is]":

Now, I know this is confusing, sort of a mind tongue twister. The objective is to make clear to yourself what your unconscious mind is trying to do, so you can defuse it. You are acknowledging that, on an unconscious level, you are looking for an excuse to prove the limiting decision is true. This event you are triggered by is giving you that "good excuse." It's accommodating the intention of your unconscious mind.

~ Try saying, "All this experience is is just a really good excuse for my unconscious mind to prove my belief (that I already had) that [whatever the limiting decision is]."

> For example, you might say, "All this experience is, is just a really good excuse for my unconscious mind to prove the belief (that I already had) that I'm not an acceptable person."

Can you feel the triggered emotion dissipating? Experiment with the best words to use to reframe this, so it defuses it for you.

▶ STEP 10. GIVE UP BLAMING

<u>Give up blaming your painful, emotional experience on some-</u>
<u>one or something outside of yourself:</u>

Take responsibility for it as your own internal, emotional experience that you are creating.

NOTE: *The Defuse Your Emotional Triggers Process is a helpful tool in shifting you out of a triggered state in many circumstances. However, this process is not the same as clearing the limiting decision altogether. With limiting decisions you are very identified with, you may not be able to get out of a triggered state without actually clearing the limiting decision. Clearing limiting decisions requires professional help. The most effective method I know to clear limiting decisions is the NLP process called TimeLine.*

A Summary of What We've Just Covered

Intense negative feelings can suddenly come up in your interactions with others when limiting decisions have been triggered in you. When that occurs, you are projecting your pain onto someone outside of yourself. You have left present-moment reality and have regressed to the child state in which you originally made the limiting decision. You are in your substitute world.

The purpose of the Defuse Your Emotional Triggers Process is to help you move out of a state of disempowered projection where you believe the other person is the source of your painful feelings—and into a state of emotional well-being and empowerment, bringing you back to your emotional center. To put it simply, the purpose is to get you out of a triggered state.

Step 1 is to become aware that you are having a triggered emotional response to someone or something. This is the first step in becoming conscious.

When the triggered emotions are so strong it is difficult to follow a cognitive process, you can follow the two optional steps (**steps 2 and 3**). The first one helps you dissipate the emotional intensity, and the second helps you experience your triggered emotions from a more objective place.

Steps 4-7 clarify what the specific limiting decision is that has been triggered.

Steps 8 and 9 reframe where the source of your pain is coming from.

The purpose of all the steps is to shift from experiencing your painful emotions as being imposed on you from outside of yourself— to becoming conscious of the process by which your own unconscious mind is creating that painful experience. When you really get that it is *you* creating your own pain, that defuses the emotional trigger. You no longer feel at the mercy of whoever triggered you.

Step 10 is the culmination of all the steps in which you take responsibility for your own internal experience.

There is a Guide to the Defuse Your Emotional Triggers Process at the end of this chapter. You can print it out and have it handy to remind you of the steps to take when you get triggered.

I suggest you keep a small notebook (or some other means of note-taking) with you and write down when you are triggered by anyone or any situation. Go through this process and write down your story and responses to each step for each triggered event. Pretty soon, you will recognize that the themes of the stories and the limiting decisions at the bottom of them keep repeating themselves. This will make it easier for you to see through the camouflage of your stories and recognize your limiting decisions for what they are.

If you practice this process, it will help you get out of the triggered states you get into. And, it will help you give up blaming the triggered feelings you experience on someone or something outside of yourself. It will help you take responsibility for them as your own internal, distorted experience you create as a part of your substitute world.

The goal is to eventually catch yourself being triggered right in the moment and immediately begin the process. But since this process is training your unconscious mind to do something radically different from what it is invested in doing, it may take some time for you to be able to catch yourself in the moment. You may think of it an hour or two later. Then the next time, it will be a little closer to the actual time of the event.

If this comes up with a person you are close with, in most cases, it's best to acknowledge to him that you are triggered and explain that you need some space to work through it. Even just acknowledging you are triggered can defuse the situation or shift the energy in it.

This might come up, however, with someone you do not feel comfortable letting know you are triggered. If that is the case, just becoming aware that you are triggered and need to work on it can help you get through the moment until you have time to yourself to go through the process.

Doing this exercise and becoming conscious of what your unconscious mind is doing can help you understand how subjective your experience of reality is. You can also experience the investment the unconscious mind has in proving the limiting decision is true.

A Review of a Triggered Scenario

Let's review the scenario from the last chapter in which Amanda and Andrew were in conflict with each other and reacting to each other from a triggered place.

In that scenario, Amanda and Andrew were each invested in proving that they were right and the other was wrong, they were each holding in place a particular story, and they were each trying to prove that their story is true.

Now let's review that same scenario, but in this version, they use the Defuse Your Emotional Triggers Process.

If Amanda and Andrew really wanted to solve the conflict between them, they would each have to be willing to let go of their investment in their story.

Using the Defuse Your Emotional Triggers Process, they could each focus in on what limiting decisions are being triggered in them. Amanda could recognize she has the limiting decision that she's incapable, and Andrew could recognize that he has the limiting decision that women are incapable of functioning out in the world.

They could recognize that the pain they have been feeling is not caused by the other but originates from inside themselves. They could then recognize the behavior they each have been acting out that causes the conflict between them.

Amanda could admit that she doesn't pay close attention to the news before giving an opinion because she doesn't believe she could understand it anyway. And Andrew could admit that he believes women are incapable of functioning out in the world. He could admit that, as a result of this assumption, he is dismissive of Amanda and doesn't try to get to know who she is.

When Amanda recognizes the feeling of being incapable is a limiting decision rather than reality, she can do something about it. Rather than avoiding the pain of her limiting decision by putting in no effort, she can start applying herself. Andrew could then support her effort to apply herself rather than putting her down when she doesn't. They will both, very likely, be pleasingly surprised at how well Amanda understands what is going on in the world when she applies herself.

When we give up the power struggle with another person, we can then become aware of what is really there between us, underneath our defended responses. It is generally some form of love and understanding. This can open the door to thoughtfully discussing the actual problem in order to discover a solution rather than using the problem to create division.

Applying This to Your Everyday Life

The next time you get into a conflict with someone:

▶ Ask yourself if you are interested in finding a solution, resolution, or way forward or if you are more interested in proving that the reality of the situation is the way you are defining it.

If you are in conflict with someone, the likelihood is that you're more interested in proving reality is the way you are defining it. You are invested in holding in place your substitute world.

▶ Ask yourself what you are trying to prove and what you are trying to defend yourself against.

- Are you trying to prove that, for example, you have been wronged, are being treated disrespectfully, or you can't trust men?

- Are you trying to defend yourself against, for example, believing you are worthless, unlovable, or a failure?

▶ To get yourself out of the substitute world you have gotten yourself entrenched in, and in order to find a solution, resolution, or way forward in this situation, first you must get yourself out of a triggered state.

To do this, you can use the Defuse Your Emotional Triggers Process, an NLP TimeLine session, or some other resource. Once you are no longer triggered, you will stop seeing the other person as a symbol you need to control in order to hold in place your substitute world. That will allow you to be open to what is actually true between you. It will lead to actual solutions.

⌐᠑᠑ᠦ⌐

The Guide for The Defuse Your Emotional Triggers Process

1. <u>Recognize you are in an emotionally triggered state.</u> Many people have a sort of sick, familiar feeling— "Oh, that old feeling again." Allow yourself to become fully conscious of it. Feel it fully.

(The next two steps are optional. They are sometimes helpful when the feeling is so strong it is necessary to dissipate it before following the rest of the process.)

2. *(Optional)* <u>Express the emotion you are feeling full out,</u> but don't direct it toward or about anyone. Express it as pure emotion, such as: "I am ANGRY!!!"

3. *(Optional)* <u>Objectify your emotion by describing how it feels</u>—Where is it located in your body, what does the energy feel like? Try moving it around. (Objectifying your emotion helps you get out of a subjective state, where you experience the emotion as having power over you.)

4. <u>Get clear the story you are telling yourself about the cause of your emotional response.</u> It's usually in the form of blaming someone or something, such as, "That person is invalidating me."

5. <u>Observe what the next progressions of the story are.</u> "He'll never acknowledge what I mean to him." Then, "I'll never have a happy life with anyone." Then, "I'll always be isolated and lonely." (It

94

usually goes from specific to larger and larger generalizations.) Becoming conscious of the progression of your story gives you a more realistic perspective on it. You can observe your progressions getting increasingly less rational as your story generalizations become larger.

6. **Bring your awareness inside yourself and recognize the vulnerable feeling you are feeling,** apart from the meaning (story) you have attached to it and the person you have projected it onto, such as feeling not valuable, stupid, or wrong.

7. **Get conscious of the belief you have about yourself that is causing the feeling at the root of the story.** "I am bad." "I'm stupid." "I'm worthless." These are your limiting decisions.

8. **Reframe how you are experiencing this in order to defuse the emotional impact for yourself.** "I am telling myself that [the limiting decision]."

9. **Experiment with the best way to reframe this, so it defuses it further for you,** such as: "All this experience is is just a really good excuse for my unconscious mind to prove my belief (that I already had) that [the limiting decision]."

10. **Give up blaming the painful experience on someone or something outside yourself.** Take responsibility for it as your own internal emotional experience that you are creating.

—————— ꝯꙅꝯ ——————

This process brings you back to the real source of your pain instead of trying to solve it by trying to affect or blame someone outside yourself.

CHAPTER EIGHT

The Real World

The first part of this book described a distorted reality system set up to prove our limiting decisions are true. This substitute world is made up of limiting decisions, substitute personas, and substitute desires. It is the reality system we are living in when our lives aren't working.

Now, we're ready to switch our focus and explore an entirely different reality system, one in which life works wonderfully well. It's called the real world.

As I described in Chapters One and Two, we don't experience reality directly. Instead, we experience a model of reality. The model of reality we live in is formed by the information we filter in and how we interpret that information. Depending on what information we filter in and how we interpret it, the model of reality we live in is either a substitute world or the real world.

In the areas of your life in which your limiting decisions distort your experience, the information you filter in supports your limiting decisions, not what is real and true. In the areas of your life not distorted by your limiting decisions, the information you filter in is what is actually real and true. That real and true information forms your model of the real world.

A model of reality, by definition, is confined to what you can conceive of or understand. It is something you can mentally encompass. However, when you allow what is real and true into your experience, you allow in living experience that expands your perspective beyond what you already know. This living experience causes your understanding of the real world to transcend being just a model of reality. You are in contact with what is larger than you and is beyond your control.

What Is Real?

What is true is what is real.

What truly matters to you is an example of what is real. In contrast, even though a substitute desire feels real to your substitute persona, it is not. A substitute desire is a made-up symbol that is a substitute for what matters to you. A substitute desire does not give you love, connection, stability, emotional nourishment, or survival.

What truly matters to you is real because it is what is true about you. It is inherent in the nature of who you are. We don't control what does or doesn't matter to us. It exists beyond what we can conceive of and beyond what we can control.

Anything real and true (for example, our real selves, real desires/needs, and the real world) connects us to Source.

Source

(I use the term "Source" in this book because most people can relate to it. For myself, I prefer using "the Divine" because it implies sacredness.)

Source is the plumb line the real world is oriented around. Being aligned with Source is what makes the real world wondrous and transformational, with unlimited potential—connecting you with what is beyond your control. At the same time, being aligned with Source is what gives the real world, and you, true stability.

The real world is a portal to Source. That is because when you choose to be in the real world, you are putting yourself in the position of being aligned with Source and affected by It. To the degree you are present in the real world, you are letting Source affect, guide, and transform you.

The more open you are to Source, the more expanded your perspective is, and the more you have access to what is real. The more you are open to Source, the more you live in direct, alive experience, as opposed to just a model of reality.

Attributes of Source

Attributes of Source are Consciousness, Intelligence, Truth, Life, Spirit (Inspiration), Principle, and Love.

> **Consciousness** is awareness. It is being directly present with experience.

> **Intelligence** is direct and active engagement in experience that opens up pathways to what is true. Intelligence reveals Truth.

> **Truth** is the revelation of what is real. Truth is revealed by Consciousness and Intelligence and leads to Love. When everything is fully in the light, what is revealed is all that is true in the real world.

By <u>Life</u>, I'm referring to the mysterious force that determines whether something is alive or not, making it more than an inanimate physical object.

<u>Spirit</u> is the essence of Source and is Life in its nonphysical form. It is the inspiration that transcends our human experience and connects us with Source.

<u>Principle</u> refers to basic or inherent truths and laws.

By <u>Love</u>, I'm referring to a state of heart-connected bliss that lifts you up and connects you to the other.

Expressing a Source Attribute or experiencing it being expressed can give you a direct experience of Source Presence.

For example, when you do an act of kindness toward someone from a heart-connected place, you can experience a blissful connection with Source.

When you're in the presence of inspiration, whether it comes through yourself or someone else, you can feel the Presence of Source.

You can feel Source when you joyfully engage in life or experience someone else doing that.

This is true for all the Attributes.

The Power Inherent in the Attributes of Source

Because these Attributes come from a source larger than human experience, they bring us beyond our individual consciousness. They have huge nonphysical power, and aligning with any of them connects you with the power inherent in them.

For example:

We can recognize Truth as a powerful force that can cut through confusion, lies, and smoke screens when revealed or spoken. When Truth is spoken, it has power beyond whoever expresses it. Or, you could say, speaking Truth gives people power.

The power of Love is something that poets have written and spoken about throughout the ages. Through the enormous power of Love, great leaders have brought about fundamental social change in the world. Some of the more recent examples of these leaders are Mahatma Gandhi, Martin Luther King, and Nelson Mandela.

Someone who is full of Life can be a catalyst to ignite the life force in other people. Just being around a person like that is energizing and life-affirming. For that reason, young children can have an uplifting effect on the elderly.

Our Empowered Relationship with Source

The predominant belief about our relationship with Source (or God, or the Divine, or whatever term you're accustomed to using) is that Source has all the power, and we are in a childlike relationship with It. However, when we relate to Source in terms of Its Attributes, we can perceive our relationship with Source from a more empowered perspective.

We are made up of the same Attributes as Source. The level of Truth, Love, Principle, Consciousness, Intelligence, Inspiration, and Life you embody as an individual soul is totally dependent on your own level of evolution. It has only to do with you and your soul's journey.

Even though Source encompasses us and we can feel Its presence all around us, we can keep expanding throughout eternity. As we expand, we are expanding the whole.

The Larger Universal Perspective We Are All Connected To

Source encompasses a universal perspective that exists outside of human constructs. This perspective is beyond our limiting decisions and substitute worlds. It is a perspective and experience that many of us refer to as spirituality. We are all connected to it, although we may not define it as spirituality. It is a fundamental, objective, stable, and true experience of reality that runs through all human experience. We exist in the context of this larger perspective that is beyond our control and, to a large degree, beyond our awareness.

We try to access this larger perspective in just about every discipline we study, whether it's science, philosophy, language, or education. This larger perspective enables us to make sense of things. It gives us the perspective to access the common meaning beyond the specifics of particular cases.

For example, in English grammar, we can be aware of what the words dog, house, sky, and man have in common. We recognize that they fit into the overall category of nouns. In the same way, we recognize other words as verbs, adverbs, or adjectives. Languages are formed from making these kinds of distinctions.

Similarly, we can recognize that rice, potatoes, bread, and other similar foods fit into the category of starchy foods or carbohydrates. Starches provide nutrients to our diet. They are a source of energy, are filling, and are high in calories. Recognizing this enables us to classify starches as an important element in a healthy and balanced diet (or to limit them if we're trying to lose weight!).

This larger perspective also allows us to access new knowledge and awareness. In any process for moving forward and progressing in life, it is necessary to go beyond our current knowledge and experience and open up to some larger pool of knowledge or inspiration. Something inside us inherently knows that larger pool is there. There is a wide range between those of us who can get in contact with that sense of something beyond what we already know and those who can't.

I'm describing an underlying truth that is always there. We can access it when we come directly in contact with what is real.

It can be found when we are batting around ideas. There is a noticeable difference when you hit upon something true or inspired. The energy brightens. It's blissful. It feels wonderful when you finally discover the truth of the matter.

> Let's say you're trying to solve a puzzle, or you're trying to get to the bottom of something. When you hit the truth, it's an aha! moment. Suddenly you are tapping into something real, some truth. It's something that exists in and of itself. It is like some pole or landmark has made itself known. A piece of reality has become clear to you.

> And then, if you have a continuous flow of these moments, you would describe it as being on a roll, or being in the flow, or in the groove, or in the zone. It's an extraordinary kind of feeling. It's beyond regular human experience.

> When you are stuck and don't see a solution, and then all of a sudden, a way forward becomes clear, that's when you've connected directly with an underlying truth.

The Common Medium Connecting All of Us

There is a common medium we all experience (but aren't consciously aware of) that is the nonphysical equivalent to the air we breathe. It is all around us, like an interfacing. We are connected by it, like a common language, a common human experience. The very fact that we can communicate with each other is evidence of this common connecting experience. We assume this connecting experience but don't really acknowledge it.

A basic aspect of this common medium is Truth.

Truth—The Foundation of Our Common Experience

Truth gives us real stability in the real world.

Truth is what is really there, what actually exists. Being truthful means openly revealing your experience of what is actually there.

We often feel we have to avoid truth in order to maintain the stability of our substitute world. However, at the same time we are avoiding truth, under the surface we often assume mutual understanding between each other about what is actually true.

> For example, if you did something you know your wife would disapprove of (such as buying an expensive power tool), you might not tell her about it to avoid conflict. At the same time, your wife may be aware that you don't always tell her what you spend money on. She lets it slide because she also prefers to avoid conflict.

We're usually living in what could be described as a semi-opaque atmosphere that, to varying degrees, is masking what is true. Some people can see through it more easily than others can. There are also times (or certain conditions) in common human experience when that atmosphere thins out and becomes, for the moment, transparent. That is when something is so clearly true that no one can miss it.

> For instance (to continue our example with the power tool), while you are eating breakfast with your wife, the phone rings. Your wife answers it. It's a clerk at the local hardware store who asks her to tell her husband (you!) that his power tool is on backorder. Now the issue of your spending is out in the open, and both of you can no longer avoid it.

Truth is something we inherently have direct access to. For instance, it is far more difficult to memorize facts that have no inherent truth about them (such as an inventory of miscellaneous objects or unrelated, dry, historical details) than to remember some basic truth that you have direct access to (such as if you lie to someone, it generally makes you feel guilty).

The Two Levels of Truth

Many people talk about "your truth" versus "my truth," as if truth were subjective rather than actual. What they are referring to as "truth" are their opinions or subjective experience. This perspective is inherently separating. It ignores the Larger Truth we are all connected to.

When I refer to "truth" or "what's true," I mean something more objective and inclusive. For example, it is true (a fact) that what you are thinking, feeling, or experiencing in this moment is whatever it is—perhaps it's about the date you had last night.

It is also true that five minutes ago, you were thinking about whatever you were thinking about in that moment.

What do you want to do right now, or what did you want to do ten minutes ago? Whatever that is or was, is the truth of what you want or wanted.

Are you judging someone? Your judgment doesn't necessarily reflect what is true, but it is true that you are judging someone. And it is true what your judgment is.

In other words, truth is what actually occurs in a particular moment or where you really are in that moment. That is what I mean by the first level of Truth.

Our opinions, ideas, advice, responses, and judgments may or may not reflect truth. Some of them may be connected to inspiration, and some may be connected to limited human perception.

When connected to limited human perception, the content of an idea could be described as a reflection of your limited perception that didn't make it past the walls of your substitute persona. You can either open your consciousness to recognizing it as a limited perception or go in the opposite direction and bury yourself further in your substitute persona. If you embrace what is true, it can lead to your transformation.

If your thought comes from inspiration, instead of coming from limited human perception, you are tapping into Source. The content itself then reflects what is true.

This connects you to the second level of Truth. You have reached beyond your substitute persona and have broken through to a larger and real Source. You can feel the difference when you tap into something true. There is flowing and ease about it.

In this scenario, you are coming to Truth from two directions—the content of the thought itself and the fact that you had that thought.

CHAPTER NINE

Distinguishing between Our Substitute World and the Real World

We generally live our lives assuming we are experiencing the real world (i.e., what is actually real), but much of what we believe to be real is, instead, our substitute world. Moment by moment, we may be in the real or our substitute world. Some of us are more often in our substitute world, and others are more often in the real world. Neither our substitute world nor the real world is a constant experience we live in.

(Exceptions to this would be if you are in a psychotic state or are a totally enlightened master. If you are completely in a psychotic state, you are dissociated from reality and can't survive on your own. You are living totally in your substitute world. If you are an enlightened master, you would potentially always be in the real world.)

Because we are generally not conscious of whether we are in the real or substitute world, we usually don't make the distinction between perceptions of reality that are or are not distorted by our limiting decisions. Being able to make that distinction is important in moving toward a life that works.

Making this distinction can be particularly confusing when your experience feels positive or neutral but still is distorted by your limiting decisions. Falsely positive responses to life can cover over underlying limiting decisions. They can show up as an overly giddy feeling, as though you've cheated life in some way or like an easy win.

Neutral experiences can be a lack of consciousness, as though you're living in a fog, buffered from engaging in life. This kind of experience can occur in areas of your life in which you have limiting decisions that are not actively being triggered. You can be just going along with events that are happening and feeling vaguely good or not good.

As mentioned in Chapter Seven, painful experiences can make it easier to recognize when you are in your substitute world. They are an obvious sign that you have left the real world. For that reason, when we get into a painful triggered state, it can end up being helpful because it provides a way to get underneath the false surface. The pain shows you where to look deeper into that experience. If you can become conscious of the limiting decision underneath that painful trigger, that consciousness can give you a way to access the real world. Accessing the real world is the way out of the pain.

Perhaps you find yourself moving from activity to activity, on autopilot, barely aware of what you are doing, buffered from any feelings you might have. If things are going your way, you might feel fairly good; if they are not, you might feel mildly angry, irritated, or depressed. You are treading water in life.

Then, if something hits you hard and you can't brush it aside (such as finding out your husband has been cheating on you or

110

that you were passed over for a promotion you deserve), you might get thrown into a major emotional downturn. This means the pain of a limiting decision has broken through to your consciousness in a big way.

Now, life has caught your attention. If you choose to, you can be aware you are triggered by a limiting decision and are in your substitute world. That awareness is the first step in choosing to be in the real world. It is the first step in going toward an actual solution.

Checking Whether You're in Your Substitute World or the Real World in Any Particular Moment

Look back and review various times and circumstances you experienced during the past day or two, such as when you were with your child when he wasn't cooperating, when you were working on an interesting project, when you were with your wife when you wanted something from her, when you were having tea with a good friend, or when you got some news you hadn't been expecting.

With each experience, notice:

▶ <u>What emotional state were you in?</u>

- ~ Were you emotionally triggered? (In other words, did reactive, negative emotions come up in you?) *If you were, in that moment, your experience was being distorted by a limiting decision. You were in your substitute world.*

111

~ Or were you in a positive emotional state, present with yourself and others? *If you were, in that moment, you were in the real world.*

▶ <u>**Was your action being motivated by a substitute desire or a true desire?**</u>

To determine which it was (and, therefore, which world you were experiencing in that moment), ask yourself:

    a.

~ Was what you went toward harmful to you, such as compulsively eating a sugary candy bar? *If it was, you were going toward a substitute desire and, therefore, in your substitute world.*

~ Or did it benefit you, such as eating a healthy meal when you were hungry? *If so, you were going toward a true desire and were in the real world.*

    b.

~ Was your action motivated by avoiding something you really ought to be doing (such as having a conversation with your husband about an expensive repair your house needs)? *If it was, you were going toward a substitute desire and were in your substitute world.*

~ Or were you doing what really needs to be done (such as having that difficult conversation and, together, figuring out a solution)?

That was going toward a true desire and being in the real world.

c.

~ Did you go toward whatever you went toward to avoid some pain you were in (such as feeling lonely, angry, or stressed about something)? *If it was, you were going toward a substitute desire and were in your substitute world.*

~ Or was the purpose of going toward it to embrace what would lead your life forward? For example, was the purpose to address your difficult emotions, connect with others, or engage in a joyful activity? *If it was, you were going toward a true desire and were in the real world.*

▶ <u>**Was your interaction with someone coming from an emotional defense system, or were you actually being present with the person?**</u>

For example, if you got into a conflict with your neighbor who has complained about your dog barking:

~ Were you invested in proving you were not to blame and that your neighbor was being unreasonable? *You were in your substitute world.*

~ Or did you listen to what she was saying, try to understand her point, and do your best to find a solution that would work for both of you? *You were in the real world.*

▶ <u>In your interaction with someone you were having difficulty with, were you relating from your substitute persona (substitute world) or your real self (real world)?</u>

For example:

- Did you react to what's dysfunctional in that person (his substitute persona) and get into a power struggle with him? *If so, you were in your substitute world, relating from your substitute persona to his substitute persona.*

- Or were you relating from your real, untriggered self (who you really are) to his real, untriggered self (who he really is), focused on what is actually true and what truly matters to both of you, in order to find a solution or way forward? *If so, you were in the real world.*

▶ <u>Were you skating on the surface of your experience, in an unconscious, foggy state, operating on autopilot, or were you engaged in your experience?</u>

For example, in the period of time you're observing:

- Does it all seem like a blur to you and as though you hadn't accomplished anything or experienced anything that was meaningful? *If so, you were in your substitute world.*

- Or did you feel conscious, alive, and engaged with your experience? Perhaps it was a meaningful conversation with a friend or some rewarding work on a project. *If so, you were in the real world.*

114

► **Were you in an overly giddy state, feeling as though you cheated life in some way, or were you present in your experience?**

For example:

- Did you finally get the better of your brother, who always seems to come out on top of every situation and who usually makes you feel inferior? *(You were in your substitute world.)*

- Or did you make an effort to experience the interaction with him on a deeper level, making an effort to connect with him and talk about what matters to both of you? *(You were in the real world.)*

► **Was your thought or action out of alignment with Source Attributes (Life, Truth, Love, Principle, Consciousness, Inspiration, and/or Intelligence) or did they align you with Source Attributes?**

If they were out of alignment with Source Attributes, *you were in your substitute world.* If they were in alignment with Source Attributes, *you were in the real world.*

For example, in an interaction with someone:

- Were you insistent on proving you were right, or were you looking for and open to what was actually true?

- Were you attacking, or were you coming from a loving place?

- ˜ Were you unconscious in making your point, based on what you've always thought about it, or were you thoughtful and conscious in your approach to what you said?

- ˜ Were you coming from a reactive place, or were you using your intelligence to understand the situation?

▶ <u>Were you viewing the situation from a narrow focus, or did you open up your awareness to include a larger perspective?</u>

For example:

- ˜ Did you confine your perception of the situation to your opinion, view of things, or what you were already aware of? *You were in your substitute world.*

- ˜ Or did you allow in something you didn't already know, beyond what you already thought, or were already aware of? *You were in the real world.*

~~~~~

Next: Choose various times coming up tomorrow or in the near future in which you will be engaged in different kinds of activities. Then, check in with yourself at those times and observe if you are in your substitute world or the real world in each of those moments.

The Parallel Real and Substitute Worlds We Live In

The real world is always present. In the areas of your life distorted by limiting decisions, a substitute world experience also exists parallel to it. At any particular moment, either world can be tapped into.

When you are in your substitute world, you are locked within the limited boundaries of its definition of reality. You tell yourself stories that support that substitute reality. You are not aware of the parallel real world.

When you are present in the real world, you may be aware that others are in their substitute worlds, but you are not engaged in their substitute worlds with them. You may also be aware of times when you *were* in your substitute world. But when you are in the real world, the substitute world isn't real to you.

Here's a scenario in which these two parallel world realities have the potential to take place:

Let's say you host a women's support group once a month at your home. In the meetings, the women share sensitive experiences, so privacy is important to them. You've asked your husband to avoid being in the areas of the house where he might overhear the discussions. That means him not coming into the kitchen and not sitting in the living room for an hour and a half on those Sunday afternoons.

Your husband generally has been respectful of this. But on this particular Sunday, he was still sitting in the living room, reading, facing the front door where the women would soon be coming in. You were getting nervous about it and asked him if he was planning to stay there.

He got offended and asked, "Have I ever jeopardized your meetings? I live here too!" He seemed to be intending to stay there when the women came in. This upset you because that would ruin the meeting.

Here are the parallel reality experiences in this scenario:

The Substitute World Reality Experience

When the conflict occurred, you and your husband were each experiencing a reality defined by your substitute worlds.

> In your substitute world, your story was he attacked you, was being irrational, and was threatening to harm something important to you. In your husband's substitute world, his story was you don't respect him, you don't appreciate him accommodating your meetings, and you treat him as if he doesn't have the right to exist in his own home. Each of you experienced the other as trying to take the power.

> Your story was held in place by limiting decisions, such as you are powerless, you don't matter, and people can't be trusted. His story was held in place by limiting decisions, such as he is not wanted, he doesn't matter, and he's not worthy of respect.

As long as each of you remained emotionally triggered, you were each living in a painful, substitute world story defined by your limiting decisions. You were each viewing yourself in a weak, childlike position and the other as having the power.

The Real-World Reality Experience

This reality experience is what was actually true in that moment. In the real world, neither of you can nor would want to take power over the other because each of you is present to your own empowerment.

118

The real-world experience is a framework and perspective that includes and embraces both of you. Both of your true desires and needs are included in this reality. Therefore, both of you would be open to what each other truly desires rather than feel the need to get into a power struggle about it.

> If you recognized your husband's true desires, such as for acknowledgment and appreciation, there would be no need for conflict. You might acknowledge to him that you are aware that when you have your meetings, it inconveniences him. You might appreciate him for being willing to avoid areas of the house he would normally use during those times.

> Your husband might acknowledge you for the value your meetings hold and appreciate your acknowledgment of him. The two of you might also agree that the meetings won't last later than the agreed-upon time so your husband can get into the kitchen.

> Neither of you would wish to attack the other because you would both feel included and embraced by the reality experience you both are living in. You would both feel on the same side.

Now you might wonder what would happen if you were in the real world, but your husband was in his substitute world. He might not be so agreeable.

In everyday life, things are not as simple as they would be if we were all completely in the real world. If, in any particular situation, you are in the real world (i.e., your experience isn't being distorted by limiting decisions), and someone who is interacting with you is in his substitute world, things can get challenging.

However, if you relate to that person from undistorted, present-moment experience, you are relating to his real self and real desires. As a result, you are including his real self and desires in how you approach the situation. You are, therefore, far more likely to find a way forward that includes him.

In any moment, you can choose to be in either reality. It's up to you.

CHAPTER TEN

Life Is for Us

Truth, from the perspective of our substitute persona, is defined by the limiting decisions we have made. Our substitute persona believes the truth is, for example, that we are a failure, unlovable, bad, or not safe. We, therefore, believe truth is against us.

But because limiting decisions are constructs, they are not truth. Truth, as defined by our real selves in the real world, is what actually exists in our lives. To come into the real world, we must open up to and allow into our lives what is actually true.

This feels like a giant risk to the substitute persona aspect of ourselves. To be willing to open ourselves to what is true, we have to really *get* that truth is *for* us, not against us. Since truth is defined by what actually exists in life, that also means really getting that the nature of life is for, not against, us.

How Do You Know Life Is for You?

Have you noticed that when you do something that benefits you, your life works better than if you do something that might *feel* good in the moment but isn't actually good for you? That is because life is set up so that what truly benefits you leads your life forward, and what harms you leads your life backward.

For example, when you go to the gym and work out regularly, you feel better and have more energy. If you drop going to the gym, stay home, and eat ice cream instead, it might feel good in the moment, but you end up gaining weight, feeling sluggish, and your cholesterol starts going up.

What I'm describing is the difference between real and substitute desires. Your real desires benefit you, and your substitute desires are usually harmful to you and lead you backward.

Expanding on examples of substitute desires given in Chapter Six, your substitute desire might be excessively drinking alcohol to block out the feeling that who you are is not okay. But doing that harms your liver and causes you to behave in ways you later regret. Or your substitute desire might be eating foods that feel comforting and that substitute for emotional nourishment but are bad for your health and cause you to gain weight. Or it might be continually trying to bully someone you are in a relationship with in order to feel powerful, which then leads to losing the relationship.

What you truly desire is what actually benefits you. Moving toward true self-interest, such as moving toward love in relationships or developing areas of your life that are truly fulfilling and lead to joy—these lead your life forward. They lead, for example, to relationships that work and to finding your life's purpose.

Self-Interest and Our Inherent Goodness

Many of us have a negative reaction to the idea of self-interest, believing it is generally at the expense of someone else. That has to do with our confusion between substitute and real desires.

Distinguishing between Our Substitute Desires and Our True Self-Interest

Substitute desires can often be addictive because they give you a momentary high or sense of satisfaction. Actual addictions, such as substance abuse, gambling, compulsive sex, or compulsive overeating fall into this category too. They are addictive because more and more of the substitute desire is required to maintain the high or sense of satisfaction. Obtaining these can become the focus of your life. For that reason, we often associate our substitute desires with immorality, weakness, or a lack of self-discipline. They usually end up being harmful to us and others.

When many religious perspectives or spiritual philosophies define human self-interest, they are referring to these substitutes, as if the substitutes define the nature of human desires. When these philosophies advocate that we control or let go of our desires, they group real and substitute desires together, as if they are the same thing. Most of us have made the same misinterpretation about our human desires or self-interest.

But it doesn't mean that at all. The problem is not what we actually desire; it's going after the substitutes for what we desire. If you get down to what you truly desire, it is never something that is against anyone.

The issue isn't *what* you desire; it's *why* you desire it. If the reason you desire it is a part of an emotional defense system, then it is not what you truly desire. It's a substitute desire. Your motive for going toward it is to avoid or compensate for a limiting decision you are afraid is true, such as that you are unlovable or not good enough. For that reason, going toward it would have negative consequences because your motive is to defend yourself against what you're afraid is true.

> Let's say you always choose the movies you and your wife go to because that makes you feel in control. This would be acting out of an emotional defense system. The limiting decision you believe to be true (that you are trying to avoid) might be that you are powerless in your relationships. For that reason, you would feel you have to always be in control in order to feel powerful. This is likely to have a negative effect on your wife and on your relationship with her.

(If you are coming from an emotional defense system and, therefore, are not aligned with truth, that doesn't mean you're bad. It just means your perception of what is in your self-interest is distorted. The distortion of reality is the problem, and that is not a moral issue. It is a part of our soul's journey to undistort our experience of reality.)

If what you desire is what you truly desire, then it is a part of truth and, therefore, it cannot be harmful.

> Let's say that instead of the first scenario, the reason you always choose the movies you and your wife go to is that yours is a new marriage, and your wife is trying to learn more about you and what you like. In that case, the process of choosing movies would not be a power struggle between you and would not cause separation. That's because you're going toward truth (i.e., what is true between you and your wife), not defending yourself from it.

On the one hand, most of us have no (or very little) awareness of how much our perception of reality is distorted and how much we live and form our perception of reality from an upside-down and unreal perspective. On the other hand, few of us recognize the inherent goodness of the human soul. The truth is who we inherently are is total goodness, not *in spite* of our self-interest but *because* of it.

Self-interest is pivotal to understand because our perspective on it defines whether we live in a substitute, upside-down world or in the real world. A world in which we don't believe we can or should have what we really desire is a substitute world. In this substitute world, our desires become diverted to symbols for what we desire (i.e., substitute desires) rather than the real thing. Going toward these symbols is what causes harmful results.

In contrast, a world based on what we truly desire (our true self-interest) can only lead to love, connection, and meaning—everything true and real.

The Importance of True Self-Interest

The life of every organism must be based on true self-interest. Every moment of our lives is based on it—breathing, eating, sleeping, loving, connecting with others. A plant turns toward the sun to get the nourishment it needs. Its flourishing gives us pleasure. If it were to deny itself what it needs to do well, would we think it was being virtuous? The very nature of life is based on self-interest.

Your true self-interest defines you and is the expression of who you are. When you allow yourself to move toward your true self-interest, you contribute who you are to the world. You are revealing the piece of creation that you represent.

When you give a friend a heartfelt embrace, you are revealing who you are, receiving what you desire, and offering a gift to your friend. The same is true when you express a talent or passion you have, such as creating music, planting a garden, or just doing whatever you love to do. Or maybe it's just talking to your roommate about how you'd like your shared living quarters organized. Maybe it's suggesting a restaurant you want to go to.

Or it might be revealing how you feel about something even though you know it might make someone feel uncomfortable. (The challenge here would be to make sure you are not doing this from a defended or triggered place. If you are motivated by an emotional defense system—you are going toward a substitute desire rather than true desire.)

In early childhood, before you made many limiting decisions and before you started building your defended substitute persona and substitute world, you were living in a state of true self-interest, i.e., what really benefited you. As is the case with most young children, your focus was on the immediacy of life. You were led by what mattered to you. That is what guided your every moment—opening up your experience and development. You were participating in living, flowing experience.

You are ALWAYS doing what you perceive as self-interest, even if it's denying your self-interest in order to be (what you believe to be) virtuous. The reason you would do this is that it makes you feel better about yourself. If doing what you believe to be virtuous ended up making you feel bad about yourself, you wouldn't do it.

Those who are the most disconnected from their own most basic self-interest end up acting in ways that are the most distorted and dysfunctional. This results in out-of-control behavior, under the radar of consciousness.

For example, people who are immersed in repressive, religious dogma may not find (what they consider to be) legitimate outlets for their human desires. This often comes up with sexual desires. As a result, they deny their legitimate sexual desires. Since their real sexual desires still exist, they end up expressing these desires outside of their conscious acknowledgment. For instance, they may tend to act out sexually dysfunctional and destructive behavior in situations where they think it can remain hidden or not talked about, such as molesting children.

It is not possible to deny your self-interest. It *will* be expressed in some form, either in its pure form or, as a result of being denied, in its distorted form. In its distorted form, it is likely to be destructive.

~~~~~

The way to enlightenment is not a denial of your true
self-interest and desires. It is the recognition and
embracing of the truth of what they are.
It is coming into experience, not avoiding it.

This means realizing that the nature of life is positive.
If you come into what is true, it leads you to
the highest good of all concerned.

~~~~~

The Inclusive Picture of Truth

Going toward your true self-interest benefits rather than conflicts with others because everyone's true desires and needs are a part of the whole of Truth. Our true needs and desires are elements in what makes up the larger picture of what is true. They each contribute to, expand, and clarify the larger picture.

When there are conflicts between people and life appears not to be working, uncovering each party's true self-interest is essential to find a resolution and for life to work. This requires exploring the truth of what is actually going on between them.

For example:

> Lucy and Jim are in a relationship. Even though many painful conflicts keep coming up between them, Lucy feels strongly invested in the relationship. Jim, on the other hand, no longer wants to be in the relationship because it feels too painful to him. It appears that their desires and needs for the relationship are in opposition to each other.

> If both are interested in exploring the truth of what is actually going on between them, what is true will open up what works for them both. To do that, let's say they go to therapy, which helps them recognize the emotional defense systems they are acting out against each other.

> Lucy recognizes she clings onto her relationship with Jim in order to feel safe in life. Because she depends on him as her source of safety, she ends up trying to control what he does.

> Jim recognizes he avoids intimacy with Lucy because he associates intimacy with being controlled. He recognizes

that when Lucy tries to cling onto him, he pulls back even more because he's afraid of being controlled. This makes Lucy feel even more insecure, and she tries to control him even more.

Jim and Lucy could recognize that their emotional defense systems are so painful to each other that those systems cause them to avoid truly being present with each other. This makes it difficult to know what the actual potential of the relationship is.

The limiting decision that causes Lucy to feel she isn't safe might be "I can't support myself." The limiting decision that causes Jim to associate being emotionally intimate with being controlled might be "I am responsible for what others need." If Lucy releases her limiting decision, she will stop clinging to Jim as a symbol of her safety. If Jim releases his limiting decision, he will stop experiencing being intimate with Lucy as putting him in danger of being controlled and will stop rejecting her.

Each might have other limiting decisions, such as being unlovable, unwanted, or unacceptable. These limiting decisions have caused them to be afraid of and avoid what is true between them. They have been afraid that if what is true is revealed, they will be rejected by the other in some way and will not receive what they desire.

However, limiting decisions are never true. Therefore, when they release these limiting decisions, Jim and Lucy can stop being afraid of and stop avoiding what is actually true between them. Opening up to what is true expands each of their perspectives to include rather than exclude who each other really is, how they actually feel toward each other, and what truly matters to each of them.

A way forward can emerge only when the truth of who each of them is and what's important to each of them is in the picture. The truth that is uncovered might end up redefining the relationship between them altogether.

Regardless of what is uncovered, it is only through opening up to what is true that a way forward can be found. That is the only way love and fulfillment in life can be found, whether they end up being together or not.

Life works wonderfully well as a natural outcome when we align with what is true. It's the distortions of truth that cause life not to work.

The Transformational Potential of Truth

The process of revealing truth can be challenging. It can bring you outside of your comfort zone. But you might also notice that avoiding being truthful keeps you from engaging in life in ways that could move your life forward. It can limit the possibilities for your relationships and your personal growth. It can keep your life from expanding and growing beyond the limited way you may now conceive of it.

Here's an example of what I mean:

> Recently, Tom was involved in an investment deal with a broker he didn't know well. Tom's regular broker advised him that he shouldn't trust this new broker. But Tom wasn't sure, and he hadn't gotten enough information for himself to know if there was any problem with this new broker.

The first step for Tom would be to find out the facts. Are there significant complaints against this new broker?

Tom was afraid to find out what the truth was about this broker. That's because if there were no significant complaints, Tom would have to decide whether to take some money out of the investments his old broker was handling. If he took some money out, that might offend his old broker, who he really likes. This could also cause conflict with his wife, who is against him dealing with the new broker.

Truth often causes us to do things we would rather not engage in because they threaten the defenses of our substitute world. The degree to which we allow truth into our lives generally determines how much we are participating in the evolutionary process of change and growth. It determines whether or not we open up to the potential that life holds for us and for the other people involved.

In any situation, you have a piece of a larger puzzle that includes more than just you. Whatever Tom decides to do will affect the other people in this situation. The closer Tom gets to what is really true, the more accurate the information is that he will give to the other people involved.

For example, if Tom decides not to go with the new broker because of negative information he finds out and tells him, this gives the broker reality information. Perhaps this young broker has been getting by through charming his clients to make up for some deficiencies he has. Tom giving this broker the truth of why he decided not to go with him could give the young broker the awareness that charming clients doesn't work as well as he thought.

On the other hand, if the truth turns out that there aren't any significant complaints against this new broker, Tom will then have to decide whether to work with him. That decision would be overly influenced by Tom's fear of conflict with his wife and regular broker.

Tom's fear of conflict stems from limiting decisions he has (such as "self-interest is wrong," "I can't trust my own perception," or "I am powerless"). This situation presents him with the opportunity to face the limiting decisions brought up by this potential conflict and personally evolve.

Tom could choose to block this opportunity to evolve by avoiding finding out the truth about the broker. That would keep him relatively comfortable. If he avoids finding out the truth, he would be keeping himself in his substitute world in that area of his life.

Or Tom could go outside his comfort zone and choose to step into what is true (the real world), to whatever degree he can. This could allow him to take advantage of the potential benefit this new broker might have to offer, which was the impetus for this experience in the first place.

As you can see, truth can cause transformation by butting us up against our limiting decisions and their emotional defense systems, thereby challenging our substitute world. Truth can bring us into the real world.

Substitute Desires versus True Self-Interest

Substitute Desires:	True Self-Interest:
are what matters to your substitute persona.	is what matters to your real self.
are anything (such as food, gambling, shopping, sex, drugs, or work) when used to avoid what you really desire.	is whatever connects you with what truly matters to you, such as love, joy, health, life, empowerment, abundance, and fulfillment.
are ways to avoid engaging and moving forward in life. They disconnect you from life.	engages you, moves you forward, and connects you to life.
are used to avoid the present moment.	brings you into the present moment.
often cause conflict between you and others.	connects you with others.
Following your substitute desires leads you away from what truly matters to you, away from your purpose in life, and away from succeeding in reality in your life.	Following your true self-interest leads your life forward toward truly succeeding in reality. It connects you to your true empowerment.

CHAPTER ELEVEN

Bringing Yourself into the Present Moment

The last chapter described how coming into what is true is an important step in bringing us out of our substitute world and into the real world, where life works. Chapter Seven described the importance of getting yourself out of a triggered state in making this shift and gave you a process for helping you do that. Bringing yourself into the present moment is another crucial step in this process. It is fundamental for coming into the real world.

Being in the present moment means being present with where you really are. It is direct experience, as opposed to an interpretation or a made-up story about what is happening. When you are in your present-moment experience, you are in a state of conscious awareness.

Avoiding the present moment is what keeps us in an un-conscious state. It is what keeps us caught up in our emotional defense systems and at the mercy of our limiting decisions. It's what keeps us in our substitute world.

When you shift from an unconscious state to being in conscious, present-moment experience, you are shifting from your substitute world into the real world.

The way to come into the present moment is to start with wherever you are really at in a particular moment. Being in touch with what you are feeling is a good way to begin accessing that.

Bring Yourself into the Present Moment by Being Aware of What You Are Feeling

We often dissociate ourselves from what we feel when the emotional pain of a limiting decision gets triggered. We do this by projecting that the source of the pain is someone or something outside of us.

> Let's say Cindy has a limiting decision that she's not good enough. This feeling gets triggered whenever a younger family member asks someone else for advice instead of her. When this happens, she experiences the source of feeling not good enough as coming from the person who triggered the feeling in her. Since she thinks the source of the pain is that person, she focuses on him as if he contains the solution. She thinks she can get rid of her pain by proving herself to him or by discounting him.

When you focus on a person outside yourself as the source of your pain, rather than recognizing that the pain comes from limiting decisions inside yourself, you have left present-moment reality. You have entered a defended substitute world.

Blaming your painful experience on someone causes a separation between you and him and isolates you in an unreal world. You are perceiving the conflict in a way that causes you to move away from a solution rather than toward it.

If, however, you focus in on your painful emotion for the purpose of becoming aware of the limiting decision at the bottom of it, your whole experience can radically shift.

In this case, Cindy could be present with feeling not good enough rather than divert that feeling into a power struggle with her relative. She could then become aware that this feeling comes from inside her and that she is in a triggered state. This would bring her to where she actually is. It would bring her into the present moment. (Practicing the Defuse Your Emotional Triggers Process could help her become aware of when she is triggered and help her sort out what limiting decisions have been triggered.)

This is a much more empowered state because it is in the present moment that Cindy can actually transform her experience. Realizing she is triggered, she can choose to find a way to get herself out of that state (such as the Defuse Triggers Process).

When Cindy is no longer triggered, she can come into the present moment with her relative about the issue. She can be open to what is true rather than be in a power struggle with him about it. She could ask, for example, why he asked someone else for advice and not her. She could then get some reality feedback.

That feedback might be that he thought the person he asked instead of her had experienced something similar, so she seemed the logical person to ask. Or it might be that when he has asked Cindy for advice in the past, even though he benefited from her knowledge about the subject, she tended to go into more details than he wanted.

As a result, Cindy would find out that her relative's motive for asking someone else had nothing to do with her not being good enough. She could also realize that when he asks a question, what he really wants is basic information, not a lot of details. This will enable Cindy to relate to him in a more satisfying way for both of them in the future. Cindy has chosen to come into the real world rather than hold in place her substitute, separating world.

Try This Out for Yourself

▶Think back to a time when you felt hurt by something someone said or did to you. You blamed her for causing you the pain you felt. (Choose something you still feel triggered by when you think about it.)

When you blamed her, you were unconsciously dissociating yourself from the emotions triggered in you in order to try to remove yourself from that pain. In doing so, you were removing yourself from your present-moment experience.

To come back into your present-moment experience:

1. *Recognize you are in a triggered state and do the Defuse Your Emotional Triggers Process using this event.*

Let the process make conscious for you that you are diverting the pain of your limiting decision onto that other person.

2. *When the trigger is defused, you will find you are no longer invested in experiencing that person as the origin of your pain.*

This can enable you to come into the present moment with her and relate to her as she really is. This can open a positive way forward with her.

Because you have come into the present moment with your emotions, you have now allowed them to move you toward healing rather than conflict. You have allowed your emotions to bring you into the real world, where life actually works.

NOTE: Keep in mind that becoming conscious of what your unconscious mind is doing to hold your limiting decisions in place takes practice and growth. Don't be discouraged if you can't do it right away. Also, some triggers are easier to defuse than others, depending on how identified you are with the limiting decisions at their source.

When the emotions you feel are positive, non-triggered emotions (such as love, joy, or fulfillment), they come from directly engaging in life. They automatically connect you to the present moment.

There are other ways to come into the present moment. The following segments describe three of them.

NOTE: As you explore these, keep in mind that you might feel unconscious resistance to making the shift into the present moment. That is because the unconscious mind is programmed to avoid the present moment (in the areas in which you have made limiting decisions). Making this shift usually takes strong motivation and deliberate effort.

Bring Yourself into the Present Moment by Going toward What You Truly Desire

When you go toward substitute desires, you are putting yourself in an unconscious state. Your purpose is to avoid your present-moment experience.

If, however, you explore what is *motivating* you to go toward a substitute desire, that can bring you into your present-moment experience. Your motive for going toward a substitute desire is probably to avoid the pain of a limiting decision (just as your motive for avoiding what you are feeling was in the previous example).

For example, you might watch TV rather than finish a project for work that you really need to get done. You avoid working on the project because when you work on it, you feel inadequate. What you are doing is avoiding the pain of your limiting decision that you are inadequate.

Becoming aware that you are avoiding the pain of your limiting decision brings you into your present-moment experience, where you have the conscious choice to stop avoiding it. When you stop avoiding that pain, you can then make a more empowered choice and move toward what matters to you. You are now in the real world.

Try This Out:

▶ Remember a recent time when you did something, bought something, or went toward something that was a substitute desire:

> Let's say yesterday evening you ate a big piece of chocolate cake at home while watching a movie. In fact, you do this every evening. You eat the cake even though you know it isn't good for you and causes you to gain weight.

To shift yourself into the present moment where you can, instead, go toward what you truly desire:

1. Imagine being in that experience when you went toward your substitute desire.

2. Imagine, instead, *not* going toward the substitute desire.

3. Note what painful feelings come up when you don't go toward it. It might be feeling lonely, or it might be a lack of emotional connection or nourishment. This would reveal that what you truly desire is emotional connection or nourishment.

4. *Imagine going toward what you truly desire,* like calling someone to make plans to go out or just to talk. Or you might imagine going to some activity at which you might meet people.

> If you find yourself resistant to doing something that would move you toward what you truly

desire, then there are one or more limiting decisions that cause going toward what you desire to be painful.

5. *If you do feel resistant, do the Defuse Your Emotional Triggers Process* to get to the limiting decision(s) brought up by the idea of going toward what you desire. It might be, for example, that you are unlovable or not wanted. (Use this painful imagined situation, where you are going toward what you truly desire, as your story.)

6. *Continue the process to defuse the triggered emotions associated with the situation or action.*

You now have the option to do something constructive about the pain you are in because you are in your present-moment experience rather than a state of unconsciousness.

You could, for example, make more of an effort to socialize with other people rather than continue to isolate yourself and eat cake. Or, if this is a deep issue for you, you might seek therapeutic help for releasing the limiting decision(s).

When you go toward what you truly desire, it inherently engages you with the present moment. It brings you into the real world.

Bring Yourself into the Present Moment by Allowing Yourself to Not Know or to Be Confused

Not knowing or feeling confused feels uncomfortable to many of us. This can come up in situations we are unfamiliar with and don't know how to relate to. This can bring up a substitute world experience that feels outside our control, in which we don't know how to defend ourselves against the limiting decisions that have been triggered.

To have a sense of being in control in those kinds of circumstances, many people artificially impose an interpretation or meaning on the situation that they can relate to. They then try to orchestrate the experience from within that interpretation.

I've observed that one way people try to orchestrate a situation is to fill in the space around them with a lot of talking that has no relevance to what is happening. Its only purpose is to prevent the situation from opening up an experience they don't understand and don't feel in control of.

To come into the present moment in these kinds of circumstances, it is necessary to allow yourself to be in a place of not knowing, without imposing an interpretation. This leaves an opening for something new to enter your consciousness and is how you can gain direct knowledge and wisdom. It is how you can learn more about the real world. This place of not knowing, or confusion, is a good place to be in because it is an opportunity to expand where you currently are.

Try This Out

Think back to a time in which you were in an unfamiliar situation, and you were feeling un-comfortable. Maybe it was a circumstance you never experienced before, or maybe you didn't know how to relate to the people in that particular situation, or perhaps you didn't have knowledge about a subject being discussed.

Maybe you responded by withdrawing so as not to look stupid, or maybe you took over and tried to engage people by talking about a subject you _were_ familiar with.

1. _Become aware you are triggered._

As soon as you do that, you have started coming into the present moment because you have expanded your perspective beyond the limited consciousness of your substitute world.

2. _Recognize that experiencing what is unknown to you is what is triggering you._

You are triggered because you have jumped into an automatic, negative interpretation of what this situation means based on your limiting decisions. Your negative interpretation might be that the situation isn't safe, you won't be accepted, or you are not wanted. Making this interpretation is an unconscious process, meant to hold in place your limiting decisions.

3. *Recognize that you don't actually know what this experience means.*

It must be true that you don't actually know what this experience means because what you think is true is based on an automatic, unconscious, and untrue interpretation of the experience (i.e., a triggered response).

4. *Say to yourself, "I don't know what this means, and, therefore, I don't know how to respond."*

By saying this, you are opening up a space to allow present-moment experience in. Rather than filling the space with your negative interpretation, you are in the process of opening yourself up to allow in the positive, real world.

(Saying this phrase can also be useful when you are feeling fearful or panicky for any reason. It can have a calming effect.)

5. *Allow yourself to rest in a state of not knowing.*

When you are in an open state of not knowing, you are tapping into and are being supported by Source.

NOTE: *If you are having difficulty doing this, use the Defuse Your Emotional Triggers Process first. When doing the process, you can use as your story your negative interpretation of the danger this situation represents for you. For example, your story might be that everyone in the situation looks down on you and judges you. Defusing the trigger will make it easier for you to be present and open in the unfamiliar circumstance.*

Bring Yourself into the Present Moment by Getting to the Heart of the Matter

What's most important in any particular circumstance depends on your individual perspective; it also may be something that has a common meaning for everyone affected by the circumstance.

Getting to the heart of the matter brings you into your present-moment experience where what is true exists. When you avoid getting to the heart of the matter, it causes life not to work.

Here's an example of two people avoiding getting to the heart of the matter:

> Mindy and Sally are in conflict about a project they are doing together. They can't seem to come to an agreement, and their tempers are rising. Each feels the other is picking on her for trivial reasons.

> What's underneath the conflict is that Mindy feels Sally doesn't value her ideas, and Sally feels she always has to do all the work. They both are avoiding revealing what they are really upset about. That's where the heart of the matter is.

Being present with the heart of the matter can make you feel vulnerable when it's connected to limiting decisions we're afraid will come into the open. In this case, Mindy's limiting decision is that her ideas aren't valuable. If Mindy reveals she believes Sally doesn't value her ideas, Mindy is opening up the question of whether her ideas are valuable or not. She is afraid her limiting decision might be shown to be true.

If both Mindy and Sally were in enough pain that they really wanted to find a solution, they would each start revealing what really matters to each of them. That would reveal their vulnerability.

> Mindy might reveal that she has been feeling Sally doesn't value her ideas, and for that reason, she has been hesitant to contribute them. As a result, she has not participated in the work as much as she would like to. Then Sally might reveal that she does value Mindy's ideas but has thought Mindy didn't want to share the burden of the work.

> As they get down to the truth of what has been happening between them, they end up with the truth of their high regard for each other.

Getting to the heart of the matter takes stepping out of your substitute world and revealing where you really are. It might involve revealing emotions you are feeling, admitting being wrong about something, or admitting what you really want.

This may result in moving toward love, getting to the solution to some problem, or finding a way forward toward your own evolution. In general, revealing where you are leads you in the direction of what matters in the situation. This can be challenging and take courage as it might require your own transformation.

When you break through to the heart of the matter, you are breaking through your substitute world into the real world.

Try This Out

Take a look at some area in your life where you are stuck, such as a relationship that is important to you.

1. _The first step is to focus in on what really matters to you in this situation or circumstance that you are not acknowledging._ This might be some truth you are not admitting to yourself or the other people involved.

   Let's say you're in a relationship that just doesn't seem to be going anywhere. He is very important to you, but you don't let him know how much the relationship means to you.

   The truth you are avoiding might be you're afraid you're not what he wants in a potential mate. Or perhaps you have a negative judgment about him that gets in the way of you being present with him. Maybe you are afraid that if you reveal your judgment, it will destroy the possibility of the relationship working. (And it's true that if you reveal what's on your mind when it comes from a triggered place, it is likely to have a negative effect.)

   These fearful thoughts have their roots in limiting decisions, such as that you're not valuable or men can't be trusted. The painful feelings of your limiting decisions are what you are actually avoiding.

What's in the way of you moving forward, whatever the circumstances, are limiting decisions that are being triggered in you.

2. _Defuse the triggers associated with what you are not admitting or not facing by using the Defuse Your Emotional Triggers Process._

Examples of stories you might use for the process:

- ˷ Your boyfriend doesn't value you. Everything and everyone else are a higher priority for him.

- ˷ Men are self-centered. They only care about themselves.

3. _Acknowledge and/or reveal where you really are._

In the relationship dilemma just described, defusing your triggers would help you come into the present moment with the other person involved and experience him as he is rather than as the symbol you have turned him into. You can then more openly share what's on your mind so that the situation can move forward toward what matters to you. You have entered the real world.

CHAPTER TWELVE

Shifting Your Plumb Line

Shifting your plumb line is another crucial step in moving from your substitute world into the real world. In this chapter, we'll explore what this means and how to do it.

I'll start with a common experience many of us have—the feeling of being at the mercy of or under the control of other people.

You can take it as a rule of thumb that when you feel controlled by or at the mercy of others, it is because you're coming from the perspective of your substitute world.

> Let's say you are in the process of divorcing your husband. He has a high-powered attorney, and you don't. He is using the situation to take advantage of you.

> This mirrors what the relationship was like when you were living together. He had the money and resources, and you didn't. He would manipulate you into giving up your interests by threatening to make your life even more miserable if you didn't.

You are feeling trapped by the situation. And you are not alone. Many women find themselves in similar circumstances.

But what you are trapped by is not really the situation; it is the substitute world reality you have entered into with your husband, in which he has all the power. In it, he calls the shots and defines reality.

Now, the question is—why and how are you putting yourself in that disempowered position?

It's because you are orienting yourself around your husband as your plumb line. You are orienting yourself around him for your source of stability and what is real. Here's how that happens:

As we've seen, in the areas in which we have made limiting decisions, we believe what is true about ourselves is negative or against us in some way. Therefore, in those areas of life, we believe reality won't support us; we believe reality isn't something we can lean on for our life to work.

For that reason, instead of leaning on what is true, we lean on people we think could uphold a reality about ourselves that we want to be true. When we do that, we are making those people our plumb line rather than truth. We are making them the definers of what is real and the source we depend on. This gives them a lot of power over us and makes us easy prey.

In the case of the hypothetical example with your husband, the painful limiting decisions you believe to be true are that you are unlovable, not wanted, not safe, and can't survive on your own. You are relying on your husband to compensate for these limiting decisions.

You try to get him to do things that make you feel lovable, wanted, safe, and cared for. You do that by catering to him, deferring to his judgment, constantly apologizing to him, and doing things that make him feel good about himself, successful, or powerful.

When you do those things, you are giving your power away to a fellow human being, as if that person can determine who and what you are. You are so certain that life is not set up to work that you are using a fallible human being (and his substitute world reality) as your source, rather than what you can really depend on.

The solution is to shift what you're using as your plumb line.

Really understanding that truth is *for* you and not against you is tremendously important in shifting what you depend on as your plumb line. Doing this requires you to face and take responsibility for the limiting decisions you have made. When you recognize your painful limiting decisions are not true, this allows you to lean on truth rather than leaning on others to define reality for you.

When you lean on truth, you are connected to and are leaning on Source. You have shifted your plumb line from your husband (in this example) to Source. You are now leaning on the limitless potential of Source rather than the limited and painful substitute world controlled by your husband. You are open to the unlimited resources life has to offer.

There is an exercise later in this chapter to help you make the shift to leaning on Source.

Resistance to Shifting Our Plumb Line

Shifting your plumb line takes courage and strength. That is because the person you are using as your plumb line usually represents the original person you were dependent on (such as your father or mother) that you made your limiting decision(s) in relation to. You unconsciously chose that person as your plumb line because he or she has the same sort of dysfunctional traits as the original person.

It can be difficult to stop leaning on that person because doing that can feel like letting go of a father or mother. But you are not really losing anything. Parents are fallible, just like the rest of us. When we made our limiting decisions, we confused what was dysfunctional in our parents with the nature of having a parent or an intimate relationship. We got ourselves attached to the dysfunction.

The only aspect of our parents we can truly lean on that will actually give us what we need is what is in alignment with Source. You can lean on what is loving, truthful, or inspired in them, to whatever degree these show up.

The Only Danger We Face Is Using Our Substitute World as Our Plumb Line

In the example about you and your husband, you have been buying into your husband's substitute world reality that he has the power. We buy into other people's substitute worlds to the degree that they resonate with our own.

The real and only danger we face is our investment in our own substitute world. The danger isn't people outside us. It is the internal substitute reality we are holding in place and using as our plumb line. The substitute world we're holding in place leads to the results we receive.

In the areas of your life that are affected by your limiting decisions, this substitute reality could be a world filled with people who can't be trusted, a world where you are powerless and men have all the power, and/or a world where you have no value. In those areas of your life, this will likely result in you living a disempowered life, where you are not valued, find yourself being taken advantage of by men, don't feel safe, and/or are frequently in conflict with others.

In the example with your husband, the substitute reality you are holding in place results in you giving your power away to him.

When you're in the real world instead of the substitute world, the only danger you face is if you get triggered and let your triggered emotions pull you into your substitute world. You then would probably lose track of what is real and give away your power. But you always have the choice to recognize you are triggered, come to your senses again, and choose the real world.

Making that choice can take a leap of faith because you don't defend yourself in the real world the way you would in the substitute world. In the real world, being safe isn't about being vigilant against enemies. It's not about staying in control. You leave that behind when you step into the real world, as it no longer applies. It's a shift in focus. Your focus, instead, is on coming into alignment with what is real and true.

The Substitute Persona's Idea of Having Power

Shifting out of your substitute world and into the real world requires a major shift in how you view what gives you power and what causes other people to have power over you.

The substitute persona's idea of having power is having control. In the example with your husband, that is the objective of his substitute persona. If you engage in a power struggle with your husband, you cannot win because he has the control in your substitute-world reality.

But being the one with the control is not real power because it is not connected to anything real. Your real power is not about being in a power struggle with another person and winning. You connect with your real power by being in alignment with Source. Aligning with Source is being in alignment with the powerful forces of Truth, Intelligence, Inspiration, Love, Integrity, Life, and Consciousness. When you align with these forces (Source Attributes), you have shifted your plumb line to Source.

You and your husband have been relating to each other as symbols, not to who each of you truly is. You have both been trying to overcome the pain of the original situations, in which you made your limiting decisions, by winning power struggles against each other. No solution can be found from within that framework for either of you.

When you shift your plumb line to Source, you step out of that distorted, limited framework. You relate to your husband's real self, you relate to what truly matters to him, and you relate from what truly matters to you.

You bring the whole situation out of a power struggle in which one person wins and the other loses. You bring it into a framework in which everyone wins because you relate from a perspective that includes both of you. You have stepped into your power.

How to Shift Your Plumb Line When Feeling Controlled by Others

Let's say you feel under the power or control of someone in your life. For example, your boss is demanding more work from you but won't give you a raise. Or your sister is taking advantage of you by threatening to cause trouble for you if she doesn't get her way.

1. <u>Start the Defuse Your Emotional Triggers Process.</u>

Follow it until you become clear what the limiting decision(s) are that have been triggered in you.

2. <u>Once you get clear what the limiting decision(s) are,</u> focus in on how you have been trying to use the person who triggered them in you to support the opposite of the limiting decision.

> For example, you might be trying to get your boss to support that you are valuable, adequate, or good enough. You might do that by trying to get him/her to approve of you or by not challenging him/her.

> Or, with your sister, you might be trying to get her to support that you are worthy or safe. You might do that by giving your power away to her or avoiding conflict with her.

In those areas of your life, you are using him/her as your plumb line. If he/she acts as though your limiting decisions are true (such as by treating you disrespectfully or by threatening you), then he/she reinforces the belief you already had that they are true. If he/she acts as though they are not true (such as by complimenting you or doing something nice toward you), then, for that moment, this allows you to believe they are not true.

You are using him/her to define reality for you.

It feels to you that he/she has a lot of power over you because you feel undermined or supported, depending on how he/she treats you. As long as you are unconscious of your limiting decisions and use him/her to run away from the pain of them, you give him/her power over you.

3. <u>Finish the Defuse Your Emotional Triggers Process</u> to defuse the triggered emotions and take responsibility for them coming from you.

4. <u>Shift your plumb line to Source.</u>

When you defuse the triggers, you will stop believing your limiting decisions are true. You will, therefore, no longer feel the need to avoid truth. As a result, you will no longer need that person to define reality for you and compensate for your limiting decisions.

You can now relate directly to life, not filtered through how he/she views things, what he/she wants, or how he/she might judge you or react to you. This gives you access to resources beyond what he/she encompasses. Life is full of resources if you're open to them.

You have now shifted your plumb line to Source.

When your world revolves around Source, you have your own direct connection to what is real. This enables you to access your own power.

(Learning to make this shift can take time and effort. Chapters Thirteen and Fourteen describe in depth how to live your life by coming into alignment with Source.)

Shifting from Relating to Substitute Personas to Relating to Real Selves

When you are in a triggered state in relation to another person, you are relating from your substitute persona to her substitute persona. You're probably experiencing her as attacking you or causing you pain. It can feel as though she is putting you through hell.

The truth is that when you entertain triggered kinds of thoughts, you are putting *yourself* in hell. You are using whoever triggered you to hold in place your limiting decisions while blaming her for the pain of them at the same time.

Let's say you made a request of your housemate that she had a triggered reaction to. She reacted as if you had wronged her in some way and shot back some attacking words. She was in her substitute persona when she did that. You got triggered in return.

Every time you saw her for the rest of the day, it brought up the trigger in you that you were being treated unfairly and were not safe. It felt to you that your housemate was causing you pain, and you wished you didn't have to live with her.

What was really happening was (because of limiting decisions you have) her reaction to you brought up an aspect of the inner hell (substitute world) you live in that is generally unconscious.

When you blamed her for that pain, you were perceiving her substitute persona as a symbol that represents that inner hell to you. In this case, the symbol you perceived her as is "dangerous woman you are dependent on who has the power to hurt you." As long as you hold onto perceiving her in this way, you are holding onto that pain.

To stop relating to her substitute persona, you have to stop using her as that dangerous woman symbol and take responsibility for the pain coming from yourself. You have to shift from relating to her hurtful, substitute persona to relating to her real self.

It can help you relate to her real self if you understand that when someone acts in a hurtful, attacking way, she is in a triggered state. Being hurtful is not what she really wants. Underneath anyone's hurtful behavior lies what her real self wants, such as the desire to be respected, safe, or heard.

When you relate to your housemate's true desires, you are coming from your real self and are relating to her real self. You have brought yourself out of that painful, substitute world and into the real world.

159

Exercise in Shifting from Relating to a Substitute Persona to Relating to a Real Self

━━━━━━━━━━━━━━━━━━━━━━━━━━━━━━

Choose a person with whom you get into conflicts, such as the previous examples of your husband or sister:

1. <u>Start the Defuse Your Emotional Triggers Process</u> and get to step #4, which is to become clear what the story is you are telling yourself about him/her being the cause of your pain or upset.

For example: "My sister always has to have things her way. She never considers my feelings. She is so selfish."

- ~ Recognize your investment in proving your story is true.

- ~ Recognize you are dissociating yourself from him/her and are relating to him/her as a symbol (selfish woman, mean person, or stupid man) rather than a real person.

The symbolism you have given her holds your substitute world in place. You use your story to prove the symbolism you've given her is true, that he/she only cares about herself, victimizes you, wrongs you, and/or takes power over you.

- ~ Recognize you have put that person at the center of this area of your life and are using him/her as your plumb line. In other words, you are using him/her to define reality for you in your substitute world.

2. <u>Continue with the process to defuse the trigger.</u>

3. <u>To shift out of relating to him/her as a symbol</u> that holds in place your substitute world (her substitute persona), it's necessary to shift your focus from your substitute world to Source.

   ~ Bring yourself out of the narrow, limited focus he/she is symbolizing for you. Expand your perspective to include what is actually true about who he/she really is—what is loving, truthful, intelligent, conscious, inspired, full of integrity, and/or life-giving about her.

(In order to do this, it may help to remember that when this person acts in a hurtful way, he/she is in a triggered state and is in his/her own painful, substitute world. When he/she acts this way, he/she is not aware of you. You are just a symbol to him/her, just as he/she has been to you.)

When you relate to that person from that expanded perspective and consciousness, you will be relating from your real self to that person's real self, no longer trapped by your inner hell. You are choosing love and inclusivity rather than hatred and separation.

4. <u>Relate to who this person actually is and what he/she truly desires rather than his/her defended behavior.</u> At the heart of his/her behavior are his/her desires to be, for example, appreciated, respected, or acknowledged. You are now relating from your real self to her real self.

Whether or not it is wise to interact with him/her directly as how you perceive his/her real self and real desires is a judgment call on your part. But even just experiencing him/her in that way, inside yourself, can shift the whole power struggle framework you have been engaged in with him/her and put you in a more empowered, centered place.

In addition, if you relate to a person's real self and desires, it can open the door to solutions. That is because when you do this, you have stepped out of a power struggle and have opened up the possibility of both of you winning.

If you practice this whenever you are triggered by someone (even if it's a public figure you have no direct contact with), it can put you in a much more empowered position in life. It can shift you from using what is dysfunctional in people to define reality for you—to having Source as your plumb line and opening up to the unlimited resources of the real world.

CHAPTER THIRTEEN

Living in the Real World as an Empowered Adult

Our experience here on earth can be daunting. Maintaining our health, supporting ourselves and our families, navigating through the relationships in our lives, and knowing the right decisions and choices that might impact us and those we care about can be challenging and sometimes overwhelming. We are sometimes faced with experiences way beyond what we feel prepared for.

The last chapter used a hypothetical situation with your husband as an example of feeling at the mercy of someone or some situation. It gave an empowered perspective and approach to that kind of circumstance.

Even though you felt at your husband's mercy, you could say that situation is something you had at least some control over. What about the many circumstances in life which you have no control over?

These circumstances may have nothing to do with the kind of relationships you get into or decisions you make. It might be that a huge storm flooded your house. Or it might be your child was diagnosed with a life-threatening illness. Perhaps it was the pandemic that completely turned your life upside down.

How do you live an empowered life when you don't have control? How do you not feel at the mercy of what is beyond your control?

We are now full-on into the solutions part of this book. The first part of the book gave you a foundation for understanding what causes our lives not to work. The second part has given you some tools for shifting out of your substitute world and into the real world. Now, we're ready to go deeper.

Understanding how not to feel at the mercy of what is beyond our control requires relating to life from a larger perspective than the specific events or circumstances we are engaged in. It is a Source-based perspective that includes what matters to us on a soul level.

Learning to live our lives guided by this larger perspective is how we navigate through the challenges of being here on earth. It is how we integrate our soul-level experience with our physical, earthly-level experience. It is how we learn to live in the real world as empowered adults.

Being on Your Life's Path

Recognizing and following your path in life is essential in living your physical experience on earth in alignment with this larger perspective. Following your path in life guides you in the real world.

What being on our life's path means and what can get in the way of being on it came up in a therapy session with a man I'll call Marty:

Marty had felt in control of his life. His main focus was on his work, and things had been going well for him. But recently, he had been stressed because many things in addition to his work pulled at his attention, in addition to his work.

I said to him:

"When you're on your path in life, everything you do feels a part of it. It feels as though you're moving along where you are supposed to be moving. It's a feeling of being in alignment with or moving towards what really matters to you.

"When you feel at odds with what's going on in your life, and things aren't gelling, that's when you have a sense of not being on your path in life. This can feel stressful and disorienting. You're veering off here and doing this thing and veering off there and doing that thing. Those things aren't bringing you toward what really matters to you.

"Now where does your work fit into this picture? You said before that your work feels like an interesting pastime. Since your work is the major focus in your life, what this means to me is that there's nothing in your life that really compels you. Being on your path in life means you are connected to something that is compelling to you, and for that reason, guides you through life.

"It appears your job takes the place of your path in life. You are focused on doing this work, which is enjoyable to you and easily passes the time, but it doesn't have any significant meaning to you."

In exploring this issue, we discovered that Marty had a limiting decision that the world around him is highly unstable and that it's up to him to keep it stable. Maintaining this stability had, therefore, been the focus and purpose of his life. It became clear that he had used his work as a mainstay of this stability. That had been the real purpose of his work for him.

This came to a head because some potentially significant health concerns had been coming up that could make working, as much as Marty had been working, bad for his health. This meant to Marty that he might not be able to use his work in the future as a way to keep his experience of the world around him stable. The substitute for his path in life was no longer working for him.

As long as he could keep this sense of stability in his control, he hadn't had to deal with the underlying limiting decision that the world is highly unstable. Now that he could no longer avoid this issue through his work, he was ready to clear the limiting decision.

We cleared it, resulting in stability no longer being an issue for Marty. Maintaining stability, therefore, ceased to take the place of his purpose in life. It was no longer causing him to tread water, going nowhere in life. It was no longer camouflaging the truth of what really matters to him.

Your path in life is what strongly calls to you, and you feel compelled to follow. It leads you to what deeply matters to you on a soul level.

Sometimes we feel compelled to take certain actions because of strong inner desires or urgings. Sometimes we find ourselves exploring new directions because we feel forced to, such as to survive financially or because of an illness.

In between strong life directives, many of us find ourselves in the midst of life with no clear direction. Our life sometimes seems to work well, and sometimes it doesn't. Knowing the way forward is not always so easy. It's a matter of learning how to actively and deliberately connect with our inner guidance. How each of us taps into this guidance varies from person to person.

Following Your Inner Guidance

Have there been times in your life when you had an inner sense there was something you should or shouldn't do, or that there was some direction you should go in and not another? That was your inner guidance. No doubt, sometimes you listened to it and sometimes you didn't. When you didn't, you might have noticed that things usually didn't turn out as well as when you did.

We all have our own inner guidance. It is sometimes referred to as the still, small voice inside you. It comes from a part of you that is connected with Source.

To be aware of your inner guidance, you have to be open to hearing it. If you are constantly distracting yourself, you are less likely to hear it. But if you make a point of listening for it, and even asking for it, you are more likely to be aware of it.

Accessing your inner guidance requires shifting from looking outside yourself for solutions to looking inside yourself for them. You can still take advantage of the knowledge and expertise of others to help you make informed choices, as long as you don't lean on them as a substitute for basing your decisions on guidance from inside yourself.

When something comes up for me, and I'm not clear about what direction or choice to make or how to solve a particular problem, I ask for guidance. It feels like allowing a space inside me to open for guidance to come through. Or I stand in a place of not knowing and hold open a space for whatever the issue is to sort itself out and become clear, so I know how to move forward.

Try This Out:

▶ Ask your inner guidance for an answer to a dilemma or a way forward in some situation. (For many people, just before bed is a good time to do this.)

It's like making a suggestion to yourself or talking to your unconscious mind.

▶ Then keep a space open inside and wait for the answer to come in.

For me, the answer sometimes comes up immediately and sometimes takes a few days. Sometimes it takes more time than that. The answer can't be forced. It can only be allowed.

Don't get discouraged if you can't do this right away. It may take some time to get a feel for how this works if it's new to you. Once you get in tune with your inner guidance, it's like having a sense of clarity that is usually with you. There's a centered feeling and a sense of being in the flow and on track. It's an experience of easily knowing what to do in this moment and then the next, and what choices to make. You are connected with your path in life.

You can feel when you are disconnected from your guidance. That's when nothing seems to go right. You feel confused and as though you are pushing against resistance. You are now off your path and in your substitute world. You are disconnected from your present-moment experience.

That's a good time to stop, feel, and get centered. Look for some emotional trigger happening inside of you, something you haven't been dealing with that is diverting you from connecting with your guidance.

Maybe you feel vaguely out of sorts and disconnected from life, but you don't know why. If you focus in on it, you might become aware of a familiar painful feeling. Perhaps it feels like failure. Then you might remember that it came up because someone in your life was disappointed about something you did. Avoiding consciousness of and not dealing with this triggered feeling kept you from being present in your experience where you can connect with your inner guidance.

When you can shift from being disconnected from your guidance to being connected to it, you have shifted from your substitute world into the real world.

Recognizing Your Life Experiences as Part of Your Soul's Journey

We are always in the midst of life happening, and the challenge comes in how we interpret that experience and how we relate to it, especially when we're triggered by it. We can feel at the mercy of our painful triggered interpretations of what is happening to and around us, and rely on that as our central reality. Or we can orient ourselves around a more stable and truer source for our well-being.

Let's say some challenging circumstance comes up in your life. Perhaps your landlord has raised your rent, or your husband (who has been supporting you) decides to separate from you, leaving you in a precarious financial position.

If you feel panicked, you are in your substitute world, experiencing your landlord or husband as in control of your survival. Limiting decisions, such as you can't support yourself, there isn't enough, or you are on your own have been triggered in you. Being triggered and focusing your attention on the triggered emotions keeps you in an unresourceful state, where you do not see the options open to you.

If, instead, you recognize that there is a Source you are dependent upon, this realization enables you to understand that whatever your life's experience is, it is a part of your soul's journey. There is always a way forward if you are open to it.

Rather than feeling at the mercy of this challenging experience—or the people who seem to be causing it—you can use the experience as a way to understand what your way forward is. That is a much more empowering, productive, and resourceful way to navigate through your life.

This would be a good time to ask for guidance. You might say to yourself, for example: "Okay, what does this mean? What am I supposed to learn from this? Show me the way forward."

Expand your perspective, opening a space for something new to come in. Direct your focus toward what is possible rather than staying stuck in the impossibility defined by your story. Expanding your perspective beyond the challenging circumstance gives you more options for solutions.

Another kind of example of this came up with a man named Henry:

Henry's wife had just bought a dog, which she hadn't consulted with Henry about. The dog followed his wife all around the house, and she felt very attached to it. But the dog avoided Henry. That brought up some very painful feelings for him.

Henry told his wife he wasn't sure he wanted to keep the dog because it made him feel so bad. But she felt he should get over it because the problem was in him and not about the dog. This triggered the deep and pervasive limiting decision in him that how he feels doesn't matter to those he's dependent on, as represented by his wife.

Before Henry began participating in this therapeutic work, he would have seen no way forward, feeling as though life just wasn't working in that situation. He would have believed that the emotions that came up in him over his wife and the dog were reality rather than recognizing them as a key to unraveling a limiting decision in him. He wouldn't have communicated to his wife how he felt in the first place. He would have distanced himself from his wife and the dog. And he probably would have gotten rid of the dog, which would have caused conflict with his wife.

But when this event occurred, Henry was already aware of a larger perspective beyond his immediate emotional response. When Henry came in for a therapy session, he had already recognized that the dog had served to bring up an important issue in him. The root of it turned out to be the limiting decision "I don't matter," which had been undermining his life up until then.

In the session, we cleared the limiting decision. That released the conflict Henry was feeling about the dog and resulted in him being in a more open and loving relationship with his wife. In fact, he ended up really liking the dog, and the dog ended up liking him. *Henry had moved out of his substitute world and into the real world, in that segment of his life. What an accomplishment!*

Our connection with the real world is always there, but it is often obscured by the interpretations we constantly impose upon what happens to us in life. We believe our interpretations are true reality since that is all we are aware of.

For example, Henry's initial perception was that the dog avoiding him and his wife not caring were the cause of his unhappiness. Henry was using his wife and the dog as symbols to hold in place his substitute world, in which he doesn't matter. He had a choice of whether or not to dig his heels in and hold onto that as his reality and make himself miserable. Many of us, in similar circumstances, do stubbornly dig our heels in and insist that this is the reality of the situation. We then make it the world we are living in, oblivious that we are the ones creating it.

Henry's distorted perception had been blocking the positive, inherent potential that is there for him in the real world. That potential is the depth of love that truly exists between him and his wife, and it includes the dog.

Your substitute world is held in place by how you generally misinterpret things (even when you are not in a triggered state).

When something like the situation with Henry and the dog happens outside of your control and causes painful emotions, it can give you the impetus to break through your substitute world. It allows aspects of truth to open something more and different than what you had conceived of.

For instance, when the conflict came up for Henry in relation to his wife and the dog, this brought to his awareness the painful limiting decision that he doesn't matter. It had been there all along and had been limiting his relationship with his wife. Believing that he doesn't matter had been blocking him from experiencing the depth of love that exists between him and his wife. The situation with the dog brought to consciousness what he had been completely unconscious of, enabling him to break through it.

If you view your experiences from this larger perspective, you can realize the amazing adventure you are on as you ride the wave of life. The more it becomes clear to you that life is designed to work and that there is a Source that is *for* you and is supporting you—the more you realize that it's safe to allow yourself to ride the wave of whatever comes into your life and to experience it from the perspective of how it leads your life forward.

This is living your life as an empowered adult.

CHAPTER FOURTEEN

Finding Solutions in the Real World

Now, let's take this to an even deeper level. The last chapter described how you can live your life in a more empowered way, even in areas of your life beyond your control. It described how to relate to life from a larger perspective than the specific events or circumstances you are engaged in.

In this chapter, we'll go further into the larger universal perspective and underlying infrastructure we are all connected to that was described in Chapter Eight.

Divine Order

(If you are not comfortable with using "Divine," you can substitute "Source-based," "Universal," or whatever is equivalent for you.)

In the real world, there is an overall intelligence supporting us and keeping everything that is real in Divine Order. Each moment holds a directive, a way forward from within present-moment experience. You don't have to feel overwhelmed by all the possibilities in your life. You only have to be present to this moment.

You can still look at the larger picture and plan for the future. But you have to be flexible, according to what the present moment is opening up for you. This may radically alter your plans.

<u>Divine Order is upheld by the Attributes of Source and is the underlying structure of the real world.</u>

- Because inherent in the real world is **<u>Intelligence</u>**, Divine Order is aware of the repercussions of every action that takes place; there is a right timing for everything that happens.

- Because the real world is composed of and is defined by **<u>Truth</u>**, Divine Order is revealed by what is true.

- Because the real world is fully **<u>Conscious</u>**, Divine Order is aware of and includes every aspect of what is real.

- Because the real world is born of **<u>Love</u>**, Divine Order results in loving outcomes, which are at the heart of everything that occurs in the real world.

- Because the real world is the essence of **<u>Life</u>**, Divine Order facilitates living, breathing, vital presence.

~ Because the real world is permeated by **Spirit**, Divine Order reveals the inspiration at the heart of all real experience.

~ Because the real world is organized by **Principle**, Divine Order upholds the integrity inherent in everything that is real.

———————— ꝰꝫꝰ ————————

Divine Order keeps everything in the highest, best interest of all concerned in every moment or situation. This includes your own best interest. Therefore, if you are in alignment with Divine Order, your life goes well, and if you aren't, it's likely not to go well.

How to Come into Alignment with Divine Order

Come into Present-Moment Experience

We have all these stories going on in our minds, such as our husband is doing this, our neighbor is doing that, the government is passing this or that bad law, or large corporations are lying to us. We wonder how we can protect ourselves and each other from the many potential dangers and injustices in the world, which we have little or no control over.

We think we know what's going on in the world around us, but we don't know what these people are actually thinking or doing, or the complexities involved in any particular situation. It would be impossible to untangle the situations, interactions, and experiences around us to sort out what is actually happening and how much of what's happening is motivated from a place of truth or distortions.

All we really know, and the only thing that really exists for each of us, is our own here-and-now, present-moment experience.

Coming into present-moment experience is a crossover point or a portal to a radically different experience of reality from the stories we tell ourselves. It is where we experience Divine Order.

Be in Right Relationship with Source

From within our present-moment experience, if we wish to live in alignment with Divine Order and move forward in our lives in the real world, we must also come into right relationship with Source.

You come into right relationship with Source by following your inner guidance and responding to whatever life brings you from within the larger perspective of Source. You respond to your experiences from the perspective of Truth, Love, Consciousness, Integrity, Intelligence, Inspiration and/or what is Life-giving—rather than from the limited, closed in perspective of the stories you tell yourself about what is happening.

When you do this, you are orienting yourself around Source as your plumb line. This is what the hypothetical example was about in Chapter Twelve, in which you were divorcing your husband. It was about shifting to and responding from that larger perspective.

You had been reacting to your husband as if he had the power to define reality for you. You were making him your source. The shift happened when you faced your limiting decisions and stopped leaning on him in order to avoid what you were afraid was true. When you stopped avoiding truth, you were able to orient yourself around Truth instead of him.

When you did that, you were relating to your husband from within a larger perspective than either of your substitute worlds. You were putting yourself in right relationship with

Source and were, therefore, relating to something much larger than, and that included, both of you.

Being in Right Relationship with Source Opens up Our Path Forward in Divine Order

Regardless of our circumstances, moment by moment, we do our best to be in right relationship with Source. This allows the next steps on our path to open up so we know the way forward.

We are each on our own path for our own evolution. All we can do is the best we can on our own path. What is right for one person to do is not necessarily right for another person to do. You don't have to figure out what other people are doing and how to stop one person or another person, as if they have the power to ruin the world. The real world is always in Divine Order, and your job is to align yourself with Divine Order by being in right relationship with Source.

Being in right relationship with Source results in you being where you are meant to be, doing what you are meant to do, and putting your energy in the directions your energy is meant to go in. This is true no matter what your situation is, who you are relating to, or what challenges are in front of you.

Living in Divine Order and in right relationship with Source takes us out of the disempowered, substitute-world framework of trying to control other people. Instead, we relate to others from within the present moment in the real world, where we are supported by and are co-creating with the powerful, unlimited potential of Source.

Co-Creating with Source

Chapter Eight notes that the predominant belief about our relationship with Source is that It has all of the power, and we are in a childlike relationship with It. The chapter then describes a more empowered perspective.

This chapter takes that empowered perspective even further:

We have the potential to be in a co-creative relationship with Source. The evolutionary progress and empowerment we have gained and our passionate desires toward what matters to us are vital parts of this co-creative process. Our intentions and desires—what truly matters to us—fuel our co-creating with Source. Our intentions and desires are the truth of what we bring in, the truth of who we are. It's not something we control. It just is.

Source is the inspiration. It is the infinite, unending potential we can connect to at any point at any time. If we let It, It opens the path forward to the unknown potential in each moment beyond our human limitations.

In the co-creative process, fueled by our intentions and desires and using whatever abilities we have gained that are in alignment with Source Attributes, we respond to what life presents us. The only control we have is how we respond to what life presents. Whether our response is coming from a place of being in right relationship with Source or not determines whether we have access to the infinite potential and resources of Source.

No matter how difficult the problem we face, a way forward is always open to us because the positive intention of Source is in overall charge. The form the way forward shows up in is dependent mainly on how we choose to respond to each step that opens up in front of us. The more evolved we become, the better we are at navigating the possibilities.

By "evolved," I mean the evolution of Source Attributes in ourselves—for example, how Conscious we've become, how much we live in and are open to Truth, and how much our experience of reality is defined by Love.

The Importance of Letting Go of Control

When we try to control our life circumstances, we're trying to make our experience conform to our substitute world. We believe our survival, stability, and well-being is dependent on controlling what happens in our substitute world. This confines us to the limited perspective of our substitute world.

When we stop trying to be in control, we are open to what is actually in front of us in the present moment. We are connecting to what is alive and beyond our control.

This shifts us into a different survival system. When we let go of control, we are shifting into a co-creative process with Source. This takes courage because it usually requires our own evolution and transformation.

> Let's say your boyfriend asking you out on a date at least twice a week symbolizes to you that you are in a real boyfriend-girlfriend relationship. If he doesn't ask you out twice a week, you feel he's letting you down. You then consider this to be a problem in the relationship and try to get him to ask you out more often. To you, this would be the solution to the problem. Instead, it just seems to lead to more conflicts in the relationship.

In this situation, you're not looking for truth. Instead, you are in a power struggle, trying to make the relationship fit into a preconception you have. You are trying to control your boyfriend so he fits into your substitute world. You are afraid that if you don't control him, your limiting decision(s) will turn out to be true. For example, you are afraid it will turn out that he doesn't want you or that you're not important to him.

If you shift your perspective and open up to what is actually true between you and your boyfriend, you would be in right relationship with the Source Attribute of Truth. You would be experiencing and relating to who your boyfriend actually is rather than viewing him as a symbol and then trying to control the symbol. You would be open to finding out how he really feels about you.

Doing this would be shifting your survival system. In other words, you would be shifting what you rely on for receiving what matters to you. You would be shifting from relying on trying to control truth to relying on what is actually true. It's only through opening up to how he really feels about you that you can receive anything real from him.

If you open up to and relate to what is alive in the relationship, you would be in right relationship with the Source Attribute of Life. The living energy in the relationship is what moves you toward what truly matters to each of you. This would allow the relationship to evolve rather than remain stuck in some preconceived form that may symbolize to you safety, stability, or acceptance.

Being in right relationship with Love would allow the love you feel for each other to define the relationship rather than trying to make how you feel conform to the form of relationship you are attached to.

This is true for all the Attributes. When we open up to this larger framework and let go of the control, we are in co-creation with Source. This shift in survival systems allows our lives and our relationships to evolve beyond what we can conceive of. It puts us in alignment with the powerful forces of Source.

Co-Creating with Source in Our Day-to-Day Experiences

When we open up to this larger framework and let go of the control, we can then see our day-to-day and moment-to-moment experiences from an empowered place. We can see the problems and dilemmas that come up as avenues for growth and change within the underlying context of the Love and Intelligence that is permeating the whole real world. We are participating in a co-creative process with Source.

Here's a hypothetical dilemma that demonstrates this:

You have been planning on sending your child to an expensive, prestigious summer camp to impress your neighbors. Just before you are about to pay for it, your car breaks down and needs major repairs.

This seriously strains your finances. If you go through with the summer camp plans, you will put your family in financial jeopardy. This reality hitch causes you to pay attention to what you are doing rather than follow your usual pattern from a mindless state.

If you can get a hold of yourself and focus in on what you have actually been doing, you might become aware that you have been invested in your child going to this summer camp because the camp has certain attributes that represent to you that you fit in. For example, it has a luxurious setting, top-of-the-line equipment, and exclusive admission requirements.

You might then become aware that you have been trying to prove something that you really don't believe is true—that you are valuable and that you belong. You have been invested in this to compensate for your limiting decisions that you are less valuable than others and don't belong.

This awareness could motivate you to address these limiting decisions in yourself. This could help awaken you to what you have been unconsciously teaching your children about status versus real value. You might take a look at what kind of life you really want to build for yourself and for them.

In this example, we first see you trying to be in control in your substitute world, thinking that if you impress the neighbors, you would belong. You are going toward a substitute desire.

We then see you allowing the reality hitch of your car breaking down to jar you out of the mindless state you have been in. You instead pay attention to what you are actually doing in trying to impress the neighbors.

When you pay attention to what you are actually doing, you shift what you're oriented around as your survival system. Instead of pursuing the path of control, you shift into being in right relationship with Source by expanding your perspective, coming into a conscious state, and looking for what is actually true. That leads to what would truly benefit you and is the only place real solutions can be found.

This is co-creating with Source and could end up being a crossroads in how you relate to your child and in opening up your personal transformation.

Co-Creating with Source in Difficult Life Circumstances

Sometimes life throws us a major left curve, and our well-being and even our survival may feel at risk. For example:

> You're in business for yourself and need to bring in more money to pay for some urgent medical treatment your insurance won't cover. Business has been slow, and you have no backup resources. You're feeling panicked.

> Or maybe your husband has died, and you are suddenly on your own in the world with little financial or other kinds of resources. Your survival feels at stake.

As described previously, when we shift survival systems from our own control to co-creating with Source, we are radically shifting the way we receive what we need and desire. We are shifting from trying to control life in our substitute world to putting ourselves in right relationship with Source in the real world.

From a place of recognizing you are not in control of receiving what matters to you, you have to, at the same time, function the best you can in the world. You do what you are guided to do. You take the steps in front of you. Rather than a process of control, it's a co-creative process that opens you to solutions.

This can require a lot of courage when your survival or a major aspect of your well-being feels at risk—and you are emotionally triggered.

Here are guidelines to help you find your way forward in difficult life circumstances as well as in life in general.

Guidelines for Co-Creating with Source, Especially in Difficult Life Circumstances

These guidelines bring together pivotal material, mostly covered previously, into a step-by-step format. Following them requires focus, intention, and strong motivation, especially in the areas of your life affected by your limiting decisions (until the limiting decisions are released).

(Although I've listed these guidelines in numerical order, they don't necessarily have to be followed in that order. They also don't necessarily come in such distinct, separate steps. They can interweave with each other and can often apply at the same time. You may find that some apply more or are more helpful in some moments than in others. I've described them as separate steps to make them easier to understand and remember.)

1. <u>Change your emotional state to a state of well-being.</u>

A vital (and usually the first) step in co-creating with Source is to get yourself out of a triggered (upset) state and into a state of well-being.

Here are two suggestions for ways to do that. The purpose of the first is to bring you into a general state of well-being. The purpose of the second is to get you out of a specific triggered state:

a. <u>Bring yourself into a higher vibrational state, where you feel aligned with Source.</u>

1) There are many ways to do this. Using a breath-focused meditation, such as the one that follows, is one way:

~ Center your body.

~ Slow your breathing down.

~ Focus on your breath as it moves upward each time you breathe in.

~ Focus on your breath filling your lungs and moving beyond your lungs and up through the top of your head, as well as dispersing throughout your body.

~ Keep doing this as long as it feels right.

It feels good to bring yourself into this higher vibrational state of consciousness. Practice doing this so you can bring yourself into that vibrational state at any time. It can help bring you out of your substitute world.

2) A variation is to immerse yourself into the experience of Source and/or Source Attributes:

Source, as a whole (in addition to its specific attributes), has a powerful Presence you can open yourself to connecting with. (If you can't yet connect with Source as a whole, begin with just Its Attributes.)

~ Focus on feeling Source or a Source Attribute, such as Love or Life.

~ Fill your breath with that feeling and disperse it throughout your body. You can focus on whatever

Source Attribute comes to mind or as your needs dictate.

> For example, if you feel tired or sick, it can feel wonderful and healing to focus on Living Life energy flowing with your breath, up through your lungs, up through the top of your head, and throughout your body. Or another example is focusing on Divine Love flowing through all of you, feeling Its presence all around you.

b. <u>Follow the Defuse Your Emotional Triggers Process to get yourself out of a specific triggered state—using what you are afraid of or are concerned about as your story.</u>

2. <u>Step into your present-moment experience:</u>

In difficult life circumstances, you may find yourself in an unresourceful state, where it's difficult to find solutions. If you are in an unresourceful state, you are probably not in your present-moment experience, which is the only place solutions can be found.

Coming into the present moment shifts you into a resourceful state and allows you to become aware of resources and opportunities that are there for you. There is always a way forward from within present-moment experience.

Some of the things we do that cause us to leave the present moment are: avoiding what we are feeling, going toward substitute desires, avoiding experiencing what is unknown or confusing to us, and avoiding the heart of the matter.

What follows briefly addresses some ways to bring yourself back into the present moment. (They are described in detail in Chapter Eleven.)

a. <u>Become aware of what you are feeling:</u>

When you are triggered, you are trying to get rid of a painful feeling (your limiting decision) by projecting it onto the person or situation that has triggered it in you. This separates you from your present-moment experience and puts you in an unconscious state.

Focusing in on what you are feeling brings you back into a present-moment, conscious state.

b. <u>Go toward what you truly desire, what really matters to you:</u>

When you go toward your substitute desires, you are in an unconscious, unresourceful state. Going toward what you truly desire brings you into the present moment and leads your life forward toward what actually benefits you.

c. <u>Allow yourself to not know or be confused:</u>

The only danger about being in a state of not knowing or being confused is if you are triggered by being in that state and try to avoid experiencing it. When you do that, you have left the present moment. When you leave the present moment, you're stuck in your substitute world.

If, instead, you allow yourself to be in a state of not knowing or confusion and open up to what is there, it will bring you out of your substitute world and expand your experience. It will bring you beyond what you already know.

189

d. <u>Open up to the heart of the matter:</u>

The heart of the matter is where the rubber hits the road. It's what really counts in any situation. It's where you come face to face with what is actually true.

If you avoid the heart of the matter, you are in your substitute world. Opening up to the heart of the matter brings you into the present moment and into the real world. It puts you in an empowered position in life.

(Coming into the present moment is basic in the co-creative process. All the steps described in these guidelines involve coming into the present moment in some form or are from the perspective of present-moment experience.)

3. <u>Focus on the outcome you truly desire in the problem situation:</u>

a. <u>Make sure what you're focusing on is what truly matters to you, rather than trying to receive a substitute desire.</u>

In a hypothetical example given earlier in this chapter, you were trying to receive a substitute desire from your boyfriend. The substitute desire was you expecting him to ask you out two times a week, which to you symbolized being in a true boyfriend/girlfriend relationship.

In contrast, what truly mattered to you in that example was what is actually true and alive between you and your boyfriend and the actual love between you.

When you go toward what you truly desire, it can take courage because it means releasing control over what you experience. You are engaging in living life experience. Releasing control brings you into co-creation with Source, which generally results in your transformation.

Real solutions can only be found when you open yourself to your true desires. When you do this, it brings you out of your substitute world and into the real world.

b. <u>Keep your focus on what you want, not on what you don't want or are afraid of.</u>

What you focus on is what you are orienting your life around. It is the reality experience you are living in and holding in place. As a result, it is what you are likely to receive. When you shift from focusing on what you don't want to what you want, you shift from your substitute world to the real world.

4. <u>Let go of trying to have control over receiving the outcomes you desire:</u>

Focusing on what you want is not the same as obsessing about it.

Like most of us, you have probably obsessed about a getting particular outcome that you don't have control over, such as receiving the money you need in time to pay your rent, or receiving a reassuring email response from someone you have been in conflict with, or finding out if you have been hired for a job you really want.

Because you have no control over the outcome, (in the areas of your life affected by limiting decisions) negative expectations, thoughts, and fears can take over. They are fueled by the limiting decision(s) that defines your substitute world.

The outcome you're obsessing on has now become a symbol that you are trying to control, feeling all will be well if you receive it. The purpose of receiving this symbolic outcome is to negate a limiting decision you believe to be true, such as that you're not going to survive, you're not lovable, or you aren't good enough.

In obsessing about the symbolic outcome, you are focused on a symbolic solution rather than a real solution to the problem. The real problem is your unconscious energy is focused on trying to prove your limiting decision is true and is holding in place a substitute world based on it.

When you try to control symbolic outcomes, you are in a framework that excludes possibilities outside your control, which is where the real resources are. You are trying to make what you receive conform to the limitations of your substitute world.

The way forward is to:

> **a.** <u>Focus in on what the limiting decision is that is fueling your intense desire to receive that particular symbolic outcome.</u> That limiting decision is holding in place a substitute world in which you can't receive what you desire.

> **b.** <u>Shift your perspective from trying to control the symbolic result to becoming aware of the substitute</u>

reality you have been unconsciously trying to hold in place.

c. Catch yourself being invested in holding that substitute reality in place.

d. Focus, instead, on *opening yourself up* to life working—including receiving what you truly desire—as the general framework you live in.

> You might say to yourself, for example, "I open myself to life working," or "I open myself to receiving love."

e. Let go of trying to control the form that what you desire comes in, such as a specific, symbolic outcome.

> When you open yourself up to life working and let go of trying to control the specific form it comes in, you are focusing on receiving what is there for you. This opens you to a larger framework beyond what you control. In doing that, you are opening yourself to a co-creative process with Source.

f. Guard against being arrogant.

> Arrogance about the outcome is when you think you have the outcome in your control rather than opening up to what is there. When you do that, you are shutting yourself off from Source, and things aren't likely to go well—sooner or later.

5. <u>Recognize that even though you don't have control over what life brings, life is *for* you:</u>

a. <u>Your true desires are part of the real world.</u> The only things that have been blocking you from receiving what you truly desire are your limiting decisions.

b. <u>Letting go of control is not the same as being powerless.</u> When you let go of control, you can still respond in an empowered way to whatever life brings.

How empowered you are in your response depends on your level of evolution in coming into alignment and co-creation with Source. In other words, it depends on how much you can respond from a Source-based place, such as from Consciousness, Truth, Inspiration, Love, and Integrity.

6. <u>Shift your plumb line to Source:</u>

Problem circumstances result from orienting yourself around a limited and untrue source as your plumb line rather than Source. When you're triggered by that problem circumstance, the story you use to define it also becomes a part of that dysfunctional plumb line.

~ **Expand your perspective beyond** your immediate situation or circumstance and beyond the story you're telling yourself about what it means.

~ **Expand your perspective** beyond the fear and panic brought up by your story to the larger truth that exists in the present moment, where all the possibilities exist.

194

To do that:

a. <u>Get yourself out of the story:</u>

Perhaps the biggest challenge when you're in a difficult life circumstance is to get yourself out of the story you're using to define and distort reality, such as, "They'll never let me advance at work because I'm a woman." It's the substitute world you are stuck in.

One way to get yourself out of the story is to do the Defuse Triggers Process. Use the process to separate yourself from the story you're telling yourself about what is happening by:

- observing your investment in proving the story is true

- becoming conscious of what the limiting decision is that has been triggered and that this is the real source of your pain (such as men don't value women)

- becoming aware of your unconscious mind's investment in proving the limiting decision is true

- recognizing this situation as an excuse your unconscious mind is using to prove the limiting decision is true

(Now you may wonder: What if it's actually true that those in power at my work don't value women? How is this about my limiting decision?

You may find yourself in this position *because* you have this limiting decision. You are setting yourself up to prove your limiting decision is true. So, it's a double whammy—both you and your work are holding that in place. If you cleared the limiting decision, you would no longer be supporting it, and you may find a way to evolve your work situation. Or you may just find a better job.)

b. <u>Bring yourself into right relationship with Source:</u>

When you let go of the story you are telling yourself about what is happening and take responsibility for the pain or upset you feel coming from your own limiting decision, it shifts what your attention is oriented around and what you feel dependent on.

You're shifting from allowing the story to define reality for you to opening up to the possibilities that are actually there for you. You're shifting from focusing on what is impossible and doesn't work to opening up to what is possible.

(As noted earlier in this chapter) a good example of shifting your plumb line by bringing yourself into right relationship with Source is the hypothetical example in Chapter Twelve. In the example, you're divorcing your husband and feel at the mercy of his control.

When you, instead, take responsibility for your own limiting decisions, you stop avoiding what you are afraid is true about yourself. (A reminder: limiting decisions are never true.) When you stop avoiding truth, you can then orient yourself around what is true rather than leaning on your husband to define reality for you.

When you do that, you have shifted your plumb line to Source. You have opened yourself to resources and possibilities available to you beyond what your husband encompasses and defines.

7. <u>In your life circumstances, especially in problem circumstances, focus on the process you're engaged in in relation to each circumstance, not the circumstance itself:</u>

We usually use our interpretations of circumstances to define reality for us, as if our perception of the circumstances is the objective reality we are at the effect of. But our experience of our life circumstances is generally subjective and shaped by our emotional responses to them. This is especially true when you're in an upsetting situation or circumstance.

What matters is your moment-by-moment process in relation to the circumstance, not the circumstance itself.

How you respond and relate to each circumstance is your choice. You can respond in a way that supports your substitute world or in a way that supports the real world. Which you choose has a large effect on the experience you end up having and the outcome you end up receiving.

~ **From within your present-moment experience, moment by moment, do the best you can to stay in right relationship with Source as you respond to the circumstance and move forward toward a solution.**

For example, some difficult circumstance occurs, and you are triggered by the limiting decision that life is against you. If you get into a state of depression or fear and find yourself cycling depressing, fearful outcomes in your mind that prove life doesn't work, you are in a no-win situation. You are digging yourself further and further into your substitute world. Any solutions you can think of from this perspective would be a power struggle with life as if life is against you.

But if, instead, you expand your perspective and open yourself up to possible solutions from the perspective that life is for you, you are letting go of the control and opening the way forward for yourself.

You can't lean on your experience of life's circumstances as your source of reality and stability, but you *can* lean on your *process* of responding to life's circumstances when you are in right relationship with Source. When you are in right relationship with Source, you are leaning on the ultimate source of stability.

Responding to your life circumstances in right relationship with Source requires listening to your inner guidance.

8. <u>Ask for, listen for, be open to, and follow your inner guidance:</u>

Listening for and following your guidance is always important in your life, especially when you're in the midst of difficult circumstances. Following your guidance keeps you in right relationship with Source.

a. <u>Ask your guidance to show you the way forward in the circumstance.</u>

b. <u>Open yourself to possibilities and resources that will lead you forward toward what matters to you.</u>

c. <u>Take the immediate steps that open up in front of you.</u>

d. <u>Let each step open up what is actually there, rather than fearful-outcome stories created by the distortions of your limiting decisions.</u>

e. <u>Do everything in front of you that you feel guided to do to further what you desire and in opening up solutions.</u>

You may feel as though you've run into a brick wall or that you don't have the tools or knowledge to move forward. You may feel tempted to give up or distract yourself.

But if you keep yourself centered and stay open to finding a way forward, eventually, one always shows up (although it may come in a different form than you expected).

It may just be one step that opens up in front of you that is within your ability to do. And once you take that step, you find another one opens up.

For example, just the right person shows up or an idea pops into your head. You then follow through on whatever that experience is—and it opens up another step. It might even open up a whole new avenue for you.

f. <u>The way you respond to what opens up determines what happens next.</u>

~ Are you letting your stories limit what you allow in as possibilities? Do your stories cause you to dismiss or feel too afraid to take the step in front of you? Are you responding from a reactive or defended place?

If so, you have retreated into your substitute world of limited possibilities. (You might try the Defuse Your Emotional Triggers Process to release the story.)

Or:

~ Are you responding from the expanded perspective of Source?

If so, you are allowing Source to expand your perspective beyond where you have been, beyond the story that has kept you in limited possibilities.

There is always a way forward when you stay open to Source.

9. Recognize that co-creating with Source can require your transformation:

a. Co-creating with Source can be transformational in itself.

b. In addition, it can require deliberate therapeutic effort.

Releasing the limiting decisions that have kept you stuck in limited possibilities (such as that you're not good enough or that surviving is difficult) is often an important part of this transformational process. You may need professional help to uncover what the limiting decisions are and to release them.

10. <u>Keep yourself in resonance with Source:</u>

This is always important, but especially when you are in challenging circumstances.

    a. <u>Develop a daily practice:</u>

The start of your day is generally a good time to do this and gives you a foundation for the rest of your day.

- ~ You might begin your practice with stretches, centering, and/or grounding exercises as a way to ready yourself for focusing on Source.

- ~ Open yourself to an experience of Source or Source Attributes. Feel Its Presence.

- ~ The breathing meditation exercise given in Step 1 is one way to connect with Source as a whole and through Its Attributes. In the meditation, focus on breathing in the experience of Source and/or Source Attributes to raise your vibrations and expand into a positive state.

- ~ You might end your practice by inviting what you desire into your life, such as abundance, joy, connection, stability, or a solution to some problem. And then ask to be shown the way forward toward it.

- ~ Your daily practice doesn't need to take a lot of time. It also doesn't have to stay in a fixed form. Adjust it according to what you need.

    b. <u>In addition to your daily practice, whenever your energy and emotions begin to feel negative, such as</u>

feeling fearful, anxious, angry, or depressed, shift your
thinking and emotions to focus on Source:

You might find that certain phrases (affirmations)
help you shift your emotions and energy. For
example:

- "I let the Divine (God, Source, Holy Spirit ...)
  loving and caring about me permeate and
  transform me."
- "I open myself to life working wonderfully well."
- "Show me the way forward."
- "I'm embraced by and supported by Divine
  Love."
- "Divine Love flows through me and transforms
  me."
- "I fill myself with living life energy."

You can also use these affirmations as a part of your regular
daily practice.

c. Listen to your inner guidance throughout your day.
This keeps you oriented around Source.

Regularly focusing your energy on connecting with
Source helps you build your relationship with It. It helps
you keep Source as your plumb line in life. When you
are in resonance with Source, you are in the real world.

What I've given you are general guidelines. They are meant to
help you find your path forward in the co-creative,
evolutionary process as you come into your present-moment

experience. Learning to co-create with Source takes time and practice. It's a transformational process.

CHAPTER FIFTEEN

An Overview and Global Perspective

T he Life Is Designed to Work thought system this book has presented is not, for the most part, a separate philosophy you have to learn apart from your actual experience. It calls your attention to what you already know and have already experienced and explains it in a way that brings you to a different understanding.

This particularly applies to the definition of Source Attributes.

The Attributes of Source

The Attributes of Source are Life, Truth, Love, Principle, Consciousness, Spirit (inspiration), and Intelligence. We experience most of these in the course of our relationship with ourselves and others and have direct experience of their existence. You know when you are telling the truth (as opposed to lying). You know when someone is being loving. You know when someone is coming from a conscious or intelligent place.

Since we directly experience these qualities in our lives and, for that reason, know they are real, it is not a great leap to realize they can also transcend our individual reality experience. We can recognize them as having an existence, in and of themselves apart from us, reflecting powerful, transcendent, and creative principles and forces. Every one of these Attributes brings you into a transcendent experience when you come into the present moment with It. Each is a portal to Source.

For example:

- You have been in conflict with your significant other. When the pain of separating yourself from your beloved becomes too great, the depth of love you actually feel toward him/her breaks through the stories that have been causing the conflict. When you experience the Love that is the real truth between you, you are experiencing Source.

- When you follow Intelligence to the depth of a problem, and the solution opens up in front of you, you are accessing Source.

- When you are triggered and expand what you are conscious of to a perspective beyond the limited and defended stories you are telling yourself, you are accessing Source.

Particular people have symbolized the power of these Attributes for us. Movies and books have been written about them because their lives have had a profound impact on the world.

Helen Keller overcame enormous challenges to not only function in life but thrive. She became an inspiration in the world.

Albert Einstein's intellectual achievements are well known, and his name is often associated with genius. He is recognized for the profound breakthroughs in science he brought to the world.

Mahatma Gandhi, Nelson Mandela, and Martin Luther King brought Consciousness to the world in the form of awakening our conscience. They transformed global consciousness in the areas of human rights and equality.

We all have access to these Attributes of Source but usually don't recognize them as forces in and of themselves. We aren't conscious of the power they hold. We take them for granted because they are the fundamental material of our world, like gravity or the air around us.

Each of us can profoundly impact the world around us when we live from the Attributes of Source. It doesn't take extraordinary ability; it's simply a choice we make about how we want to live our lives—a kind word; a loving action; an inspired insight; being conscious of and being present with another person's experience; forgiving someone; revealing what really matters to us; acknowledging a mistake we made; speaking the truth when it really counts.

Acts of kindness, love, inspiration, the revelation of truth, or any form of interaction that is Source-based can break through the barrier that usually exists between us. When you participate in the world from this place, you bridge a boundary that separates the substitute from the real world.

The Unevolved Definition of Humanity versus Who We Really Are

The unevolved definition of humanity defines us by our substitute personas and substitute desires as if that is who we are and what we truly desire. For instance, we sometimes define others (as well as ourselves) as a liar, a good-for-nothing, lazy, greedy, selfish, bad, or egotistical.

But from a more evolved understanding of human experience, we can distinguish between our substitute persona and our real self; and we can distinguish between our substitute desires and what we truly desire.

For example:

> We can recognize that if someone (we'll call Todd) tells lies, or someone else (we'll call Sara) lives her life in a lazy way, these are emotional defenses against a belief that truth is against him/her or just won't work for him/her. In other words, it's a defense against a limiting decision.

> Telling lies is a defense Todd uses against a limiting decision he has that he is bad. This limiting decision puts him in an impossible position in life where he believes people will experience him as bad no matter what he does. To defend himself from being perceived as bad, he (in the form of his substitute persona) tells people what he thinks they will accept rather than what is true. The purpose of lying is to give himself the substitute desire of feeling in control of people's responses to him so he can be perceived as good. His real desire is to actually be a good person.

Living her life in a lazy way is a defense Sara uses against a limiting decision she has that nothing she does will be good enough. Because she believes no matter what she does or how hard she tries, it won't be good enough, she gives up even trying. And that's how her substitute persona shows up. Acting in a lazy way is a substitute desire that buffers Sara from the pain of feeling not good enough. What Sara truly desires is to succeed in life.

These defenses don't define who either of them inherently is or what either truly desires. They define their substitute personas and substitute desires.

Both Todd and Sara behave the way they do because they are caught up in a false experience of reality distorted by their limiting decisions, not because of what's actually true about them. What is true about each of them is his/her real self, which is made up of the Attributes of Source—in the particular configuration they're each formed in.

~~~~~

When we recognize the distinction between substitute personas versus the real self, substitute desires versus true self-interest, and substitute worlds versus the real world, we can make a quantum leap forward in understanding what reality is, and what the nature of the human being and the human soul is.

~~~~~

A Global Perspective on Our Substitute Worlds

On a global scale, we have developed to the point where we have many resources we can use to avoid our actual experience and retreat into our buffered, substitute worlds. These resources are used as substitute desires.

We can distract ourselves by constantly talking on the phone and texting; we can buffer our emotional pain with drugs (prescription or other) or by over-consuming other addictive substances, such as alcohol or comfort foods; or we can avoid the emptiness and what is dysfunctional in our lives by getting involved in the dramas of our favorite TV or online shows, vicariously feeling empowered, loved, deceived, or vindicated, as if these dramas were our reality.

Our technological advances enable increasingly less effort and personal engagement from us. You can tell Alexa to lock the doors, play your favorite music, or adjust the heat. You can work from your home and order anything you need through the internet without taking one step outside your home.

How much we avoid or buffer ourselves against our present-moment experience varies between us. And each of us can be more present in some areas of our lives than in others depending on where we have or haven't made limiting decisions. Regardless, most of us are living in our substitute world realities far more than we realize.

Our Substitute World Is Based on the Symbolism We Have Given It

The purpose of the substitute world is to give you the illusion that you can make life what you want it to be, as opposed to what you mistakenly believe it really is. Converting our actual experiences of life into substitute worlds is made possible by experiencing the world in terms of symbols. Substitute desires are symbols for what we truly desire. As earlier chapters have explained, people and situations can also be used as symbols.

These chapters have described how we defend ourselves against the pain of our limiting decisions by dissociating ourselves from the people and situations that trigger those decisions in us. We then project the pain we feel onto those people and situations as if they are the source of it. These people and situations then become symbols to us, such as dangerous man, woman who can't be trusted, or situation in which you don't have control. When this happens, we are no longer aware of who or what that person or situation actually is. They are now just symbols to us.

Symbols make our substitute worlds possible because symbols can be controlled, as opposed to what is real, which can't be controlled. We try to control the people we give symbolic meaning to and the people in the situations we give symbolic meaning to so we can receive the substitute desires we believe our lives depend on. We generally try to control these people by trying to influence or manipulate their behavior.

For example, you might try to appease the dangerous man by catering to his needs. This makes you feel you have control over your safety. Having control over your safety is a substitute desire that has meaning only in your substitute world, where you (in this example) don't feel safe because of the dangerous men that populate that world.

The example in Chapter Six about Adam and his business is another example of this:

Adam's business symbolized for him a situation that could prove true his limiting decision that he is a failure. To defend himself against that, Adam set up his business as a substitute-world reality to prove he is not a failure.

As a part of that effort, Adam did his best to impress business associates who symbolized to him power and status, as if that would also give him power and status. Impressing others is a substitute desire for Adam, and he believed it would actually make him a successful person.

But impressing others would not actually give his business a solid foundation of integrity and value. He was not focusing on what would enable his business to be successful in reality, which is Adam's true desire.

In our substitute worlds, like Adam, we believe our well-being, our ability to make progress in life, our very survival, depend on how well we can relate to, perform in relation to, or control, the symbols we have created in our lives.

You might know someone who believes that if he can bully people into doing things his way, that makes him worthy of respect. Or perhaps you know someone who believes she has power in the world if she can get a powerful man to support her. Or maybe you believe that if you can prove to your best friend you are always right, you will have some control in your life.

These beliefs about reality become stories that define our lives. These stories are what our substitute worlds are made up of.

We Get Lost in Our Stories

We tell ourselves and get very invested in many other kinds of stories as well, such as my ex is withholding money from me, my girlfriend is cheating on me, I messed up at work, or I'm going to get fired.

Our stories are often filled with symbolic emotional meanings that are held in place by our limiting decisions (such as people can't be trusted, I'm powerless, I'm not good enough). They describe and hold in place our substitute worlds.

We are so focused on relating to and trying to control each other and the world around us from within these stories that, to a large extent, we don't notice the shared, common circumstances we are all actually living in.

Our Shared Common Circumstances

Earlier in this chapter, I noted that we have developed many resources that provide us with substitute desires and allow us to retreat into our substitute worlds.

Our advanced resources, especially our technological gains, are powerful tools for providing us with substitute desires. These substitute desires are effective at making us feel we have control in our substitute world by giving us a lot of control over our everyday environment. They make getting everything we want faster and easier, with less personal engagement or contact. As a result, we are focused on more, faster, and easier, as if that is progress.

However (as described in earlier chapters), substitute desires by definition are out of alignment with Source, the real world, and what we really need and desire, so they end up being harmful to us. When this applies to substitute desires gained through technological advances, the harmful effects can affect us on a global scale, such as depleting and polluting our natural resources.

213

In addition, these substitute desires are effective at buffering us or distracting us from the pain of our limiting decisions. To the degree we can avoid feeling our emotional pain, we don't have to get to the source of the pain and do something about it. This leaves an undercurrent of built-up pain that can emerge in (sometimes devastatingly) destructive ways toward us, other people, particular groups of people, and other countries.

The advances we have made are so effective in providing substitute desires, we have become used to receiving them and retreating into our substitute worlds. For that reason, even when we notice the harm these substitute desires are causing, our efforts to do something about it are not effective (or, at least, not effective enough).

As a result, the destructive potential of what is happening in our shared world is so big, it's increasingly more difficult to ignore. Our efforts to be in control have resulted in our common global experience becoming increasingly more out of control.

For example (expanding on an example given in Chapter One):

> Global warming affects us on a nearly daily basis, with stretches of record-breaking heat, drought, floods, and other extreme weather wreaking havoc far more often than it used to. Perhaps you are afraid to read stories in the news that daily describe upsetting changes, such as the polar ice cap melting and the largest block of ice in the Arctic breaking into pieces.

> Cybercrime increasingly invades our lives. No matter how secure our home internet security systems, our financial services, the stores we use, and government security agencies are, hackers always seem to find ways to outsmart them.

Since 9/11, terrorism feels much closer to home, no longer confined to faraway countries. In recent years, we more frequently see stories in the news about mass shootings. Schools and places of worship no longer are safe havens. Traveling to foreign countries feels much riskier. The U. S. and perhaps the world, in general, feel more polarized than ever.

Our investment in upholding our substitute experience of reality is the reason humanity faces such potential for disaster. To a large extent, we are oblivious to what is real. We are walking in the opposite direction from real solutions.

I'm describing this not to make you feel hopeless about our shared human experience but to shed light on what is mostly unconscious. I'm describing an unconscious human process that has control over us only as long as it remains unconscious. *We are faced with the enormous challenges of today as an opportunity for major transformation and evolution. That's what this is really about. It is a major impetus and opportunity to shift survival systems.*

Shifting Survival Systems

We have clung to our substitute worlds and used them to gain more and more substitute desires as if that will solve our problems. But as events and circumstances in our global experience get more intense, it's becoming clear that our survival, stability, and well-being do not depend on us upholding our substitute worlds. Instead, trying to uphold our substitute world reality is what is *causing* our life to not work.

It seems we have to try every possible way to make our substitute worlds work (and, in the process, bring ourselves to the brink of global disaster) before we realize we've been

215

walking in the wrong direction and become open to a shift in survival systems.

By shifting survival systems, I mean shifting from an unreal framework of human control (our substitute worlds) to coming into alignment with Source, where we open up to undistorted experience and what is actually true (the real world). It is shifting into being in co-creation with Source.

We Are Always in Divine Order

There is a difference between our commonly shared circumstances and your individual, moment-to-moment experience within those circumstances.

Your well-being here on earth is not determined by what anyone else does or doesn't do. You are impacted by the overall global consciousness you live in the midst of only to the degree you resonate with it. You are not at the mercy of other people's substitute worlds unless you resonate with them.

And that is true regardless of how unconscious the majority of humanity might be, including their unconscious behavior toward our shared environment. You don't need other people to come into alignment with Source. You, as an individual, only need you to shift your survival systems for your life to work.

It's the choices and decisions you make moment by moment that determine your experiences in life. You always have the choice to be in co-creation with Source.

Earth, being a part of the Universe, is always in Divine Order. We can't interfere with that. What we *can* do is mess up our individual experience. But even when we do that, we always have the option to move forward on a soul level. It's just a question of how much pain we're going to cause ourselves in the process.

216

Regardless of how out of alignment you might cause yourself to be, you still exist in the perfection of the Universe. You are, as is everything in the Universe, engaged in an evolutionary process, which is always moving forward toward the highest good of all of us. Although at times it might appear we are going backward, overall, human consciousness has been evolving—at times making huge leaps.

This book describes an active and conscious way to participate in your own evolutionary process. The fact that we have evolved to be conscious enough to do that is pretty remarkable.

~~~~~

The main evolutionary challenge we face is our investment in controlling our experience of life to fit our substitute world rather than undistorting our experience and allowing it to be what it really is. When we experience life in its undistorted form, it is completely positive and works wonderfully well.

~~~~~

What I'm talking about is a large shift in understanding the means by which we are impacted in the world and how we impact the world. It's not about the people and situations outside us having control over us, and it's not about us having control over other people and situations. When you come from that mistaken perspective, you are orienting yourself around the people and situations outside yourself as if they are the sources of reality that you are dependent on.

Instead, it's about orienting yourself around Source (Consciousness, Truth, Love, Life, Integrity, Inspiration, and

Intelligence) as the source of what is real. It's about experiencing and relating to your life experiences from within that larger perspective and allowing these experiences to transform you.

You are transformed by what is true in the situation, the love permeating it, and/or the consciousness that is opening up. When you relate to the world from this Source-based perspective, you are also impacting others. You are co-creating with Source.

Making a Different Choice

▶ <u>**Imagine yourself moving through your day.**</u>

You may have experiences that result in you being in different emotional and mental states. Your experiences may be interactions with the people in your life—perhaps your husband, wife, children, or neighbors. They may have to do with your work situation or an interaction at the grocery store. Or perhaps it is some emergency that completely interrupts your plans for the day.

Some of your experiences may bring up feelings that are heart-connected, empowering, or inspiring. These connect you to your real self and bring you into the real world.

Other experiences may trigger difficult, painful, or full-of-conflict feelings. This may   result in you feeling depressed, angry, or anxious. You may have times when you are on autopilot, just unconsciously making it through the day. You are in your substitute persona and substitute world when you are in these states.

You may find yourself engaging in activities that are meaningful to you, feel rewarding, and bring you joy. They are what you truly desire and are a part of the real world. And/or you may find yourself engaging in activities that are a way to avoid or buffer you against some feeling or experience you don't want to face. They are your substitute desires and are a part of your substitute world.

▶ <u>Learning to distinguish between what is a part of your substitute world and what is connected to the real world helps you make more conscious choices in your life.</u>

The more you become conscious of when you are engaging in your substitute world, when you are living from your substitute persona, and when you are going toward your substitute desires, the more you can recognize that they don't really benefit you.

Becoming aware of this supports you in noticing and making choices that do truly benefit you. The more you make conscious choices that benefit you, the more you come into the real world where you are aligned with Source and with your empowered, magnificent, real self.

▶ <u>Every moment you have a choice:</u>

~ When some conflict comes up with someone, will you get into a power struggle with him/her over it?

If you do, you are coming from your substitute persona and relating to the other person's substitute

219

persona. Both of you are trying to impose your substitute world on the other.

~ Or will you step into your real self and orient yourself around Source Attributes, such as Truth and Love?

In other words, will you be open to what is actually true in the situation, regardless of your personal investment? Will you relate to the real self of him or her (i.e., that part of him/her that is, for instance, loving, intelligent, and conscious) and allow in the transformational gifts that this moment holds for both of you?

~ When something unexpected happens in your life that is not what you wanted to happen, will you use that as an excuse to prove your limiting decisions are true? *If you do, you are in your substitute world.*

~ Or will you stand in a place of not knowing and open yourself up to something new?

In other words, will you allow yourself to let go of the limited way you have been perceiving this situation?

► <u>**Every moment you have a choice of either retreating into your substitute world or expanding into the real world.**</u>

Which world will you choose to live in?

~~~

The Real World

It is always there, beneath the surface.

It is there when we are fighting with each other.
It is there under irritations and boredom.
It is there when we are treading water,
trying to avoid what is true.

It is under the masks of
hatred and unconscious oblivion.
It is there when the only thing that seems to exist
is misery and pain.

So real seem the terrorists, the dictators,
the ethnic conflicts that never seem to cease,
the usurped power of the large corporations, governments,
and clandestine spying on private lives.

But within it all is another reality,
a truth that exists through the eons of
wars and famines and dense unconsciousness.

In every moment, in every situation,
sometimes close to the surface,
sometimes buried deep,
often right there in full view –

There is consciousness that shines light on what is intelligent.
There is intelligence that shines light on what is true.
There is truth that shines light on what is loving.
There is love that shines light on what is full of life.

We are ever-present Divine Presence.
Where we look and where we focus
determines what we see-reveal.

The Real World of what is eternal is eternally there.
We have a choice—a world of pain or the Real World.

Which world will you choose?

~~~

Shifting into the Real World

There are two different survival systems you can orient yourself around. One is based on avoiding what is true. That is the substitute world. The other is based on opening up to and aligning with what is true. That is the real world.

Coming into alignment with what is true is what causes life to work. That's because the inherent nature of the human soul and of life is perfect. To the degree that you distort, manipulate, or depart from the actual truth of who you are and what is true in life, you cause the pain and problems you experience, and you cause your life not to work.

To a large degree, what humanity has conceived of as making progress has been to create more effective substitute worlds that give us the illusion of mastery over the emotional pain and fear we cause ourselves. We have been trying to make our common world conform to our made-up substitute worlds instead of coming into what is actually true.

True progress in the world comes from opening up to and aligning with Source. When we come into present-moment experience, in alignment with Source (Truth, Life, Love, Principle, Consciousness, Intelligence, and Spirit), we tap into and are a portal to Divine Wisdom. We bring into the world new awareness, experience, knowledge, and information that help us to evolve forward. When we do that, we are actively participating in the evolutionary process.

Coming into alignment with what is true (rather than trying to impose symbolic meanings on your experience) enables you to participate in life as it really is. You can experience the real, inspired world of Life, Truth, Love, Principle, Spirit, Consciousness, and Intelligence, which is always present. Even though these Attributes of Source are sometimes not obviously present, they are always there. You can always choose to align with them, in yourself, in other people, and/or in whatever circumstance you are in.

When you do, this brings you into the real world, where life works wonderfully well.

GLOSSARY

A Course in Miracles—A positive spiritual philosophy and self-study course.

Attributes of Source—Life, Truth, Love, Principle, Spirit (Inspiration), Intelligence, and Consciousness.

Co-Creating with Source—A process of releasing control and responding to what life presents you with while being in right relationship with Source. It is a partnership between what truly matters to you and the unlimited potential of Source, and it results in transformational outcomes.

Defended substitute world—When our substitute personas develop emotional defense systems to shield ourselves from the pain of our limiting decisions, they also start developing substitute worlds to support those defenses. These defended substitute worlds exist outside us. Organizations and social structures (such as businesses, political groups, governments, religious organizations, clubs, and families) are often used for this purpose. These structures hold in place an agreed-upon way to experience reality that supports the views of whoever controls them.

Divine Order—Is upheld by the Attributes of Source and is the underlying structure of the real world. It keeps everything in the highest, best interest of all concerned in any particular moment or situation.

Emotional Defense Systems—A wall or attack protecting us from the perceived source of the pain of our limiting decisions. The perceived source is generally the people or situations that bring up that pain in you. In those situations, as a defense, we might be very reactive, judgmental, controlling, or just unaware.

Emotional Triggers—Intense, upsetting feelings, such as anger or fear, activated in you by the pain of a limiting decision being brought to the surface of your awareness.

Inner Guidance—The still, small voice inside you. It comes from a part of you connected with Source. It sometimes shows up as a sense there is something you should or shouldn't do or that there is some direction you should go in and not another.

Limiting Decisions—Unconscious decisions usually made in early childhood. They are always some form of deciding that life doesn't work and usually that there is something inherently wrong with you, such as I am bad, I am not valuable, I am a failure, or people can't be trusted. They result from the child's interpretations of situations he or she doesn't have the development or experience to understand.

Model of Reality—Is formed by the information your senses filter into your awareness and how you interpret it.

Narcissism—A well-defended, emotional defense system. Those who have this are usually charismatic and often at the center of attention. They are good at defining reality for those who come into their circles in order to suit their own purposes. They generally put out sexual energy that makes them addictive to others. They usually attract and manipulate those who have low self-esteem.

NLP—Stands for Neuro-Linguistic Programming. It is the study of the language of the mind, how we form our subjective experience, and how it can be changed.

Path in Life—What strongly calls to you and what you feel compelled to follow. It leads you to what deeply matters to you on a soul level.

Plumb Line—A string or cord that is weighted on the bottom end. It is a basic carpentry tool used to align physical structures (such as a building) with gravity so they will be stable. We generally orient ourselves around one or more sources outside ourselves that we believe will provide stability for our survival and well-being. They become our plumb lines. Similar to the carpenter orienting his building around a plumb line, what we orient our lives around determines whether our life works or not.

Power struggle—A struggle between two or more people to gain control in a situation.

Present-Moment Experience—Being present with where you really are. It is direct experience, as opposed to an interpretation or a made-up story about what is happening. When you are in your present-moment experience, you are in a state of conscious awareness.

Real Self—Is your true, vulnerable, authentic self. It is undistorted by limiting decisions and is made up of Attributes of Source.

Real World—Is true experience, undistorted by limiting decisions. It is experienced in the present moment. You experience it when you are in alignment with the Attributes of Source.

Right Relationship with Source—Is following your inner guidance and responding to what life brings you, from within the larger perspective of Source.

Source—Refers to a Larger, nonphysical Source we are ultimately dependent on. It is eternal and is the source of everything that has real existence. It is referred to by many names, such as God, The Divine, Holy Spirit, The Creator, The Universe, or Larger Truth.

Substitute Desires—Symbolic substitutes for what you really desire (such as love, having value, empowerment) but believe you can't have. They are often addictive and don't give you anything. They usually end up being harmful to yourself or others.

Substitute Persona—A made-up self that only shows up in the areas of your life in which you have made limiting decisions. Its function is to hold in place the distorted reality created by your limiting decisions. Your substitute persona exists only as long as you hold in place your limiting decisions.

Substitute World—An inner experience in which the limiting decisions we have made determine how we experience ourselves and others. It is a model of reality we create for ourselves that is a substitute for what is real and true.

The Heart of the Matter—Is what is most important in any particular circumstance.

True Desires—Are what matters to your real self. They are beneficial to you and to others around you.

Unconscious—That which is not in your conscious awareness.

ABOUT THE AUTHOR

Jane Ilene Cohen, Ph.D. has a master's degree in metaphysical science and a doctorate in transpersonal counseling. She is certified as an NLP (Neuro-linguistic Programming) master practitioner and was also certified in Time Line Therapy® and hypnotherapy—from Dr. Tad James.

Jane is the founder of the Life Is Designed to Work thought system. She has had a private counseling practice since 1995. Her NLP TimeLine sessions integrate her Life Is Designed to Work thought system with the Time Line Therapy® process developed by Dr. James.

Jane founded the Conscious Healing Network and was a master life teacher at the Panacea School of Life. She was also a relationship and spirituality expert panelist for the Living Consciously TV show for two years, which originated out of Denver, Colorado.

Jane's articles and poems have been published in *The Light Connection, Vision Magazine, Awareness Magazine, San Diego Bride & Groom, SpiralMuse, EzineArticles.com,* and *Selfgrowth.com.* They have also been published in *The Heart of a Woman, The Heart of a Mother, The Heart of the Holidays,* and *The Heart of a Woman in Business,* which are anthologies compiled by Sheryl Roush.

Made in the USA
Coppell, TX
22 October 2021